Journeys Around the World

Mexico, Canada, the United States

Contents

Introduction 2
Correlation to Standards 3
Map of North America 5

Mexico

Lesson 1	Baja by Bus	6
Lesson 2	A Little Dog and a Big State	14
Lesson 3	Aztecs and Art in Mexico City	22
Lesson 4	Jalisco Holiday	30
Lesson 5	Reefs, Ruins, and Jaguars	38

Canada

Lesson 6	Walking in Viking Footsteps	46
Lesson 7	Mostly Québec	54
Lesson 8	Manitoba in the Middle	62
Lesson 9	The Beauty of British Columbia	70
Lesson 10	Yukon Territory: Gold Rush	78

The United States

Lesson 11	A City Without a State	86
Lesson 12	Exploring the Deep South: Alabama ...	94
Lesson 13	All About Austin	102
Lesson 14	Ancient Ruins and Majestic Canyons ..	110
Lesson 15	A City by the Bay: San Francisco	118

Answer Key 126

Introduction

The *Journeys Around the World* series provides a unique approach to social studies content.

- A high-interest story presents information about countries around the world from the point of view of students who are the same age as the reader.

- Dialogue and humor make stories accessible to the less-motivated reader.

- Photographs reinforce the text.

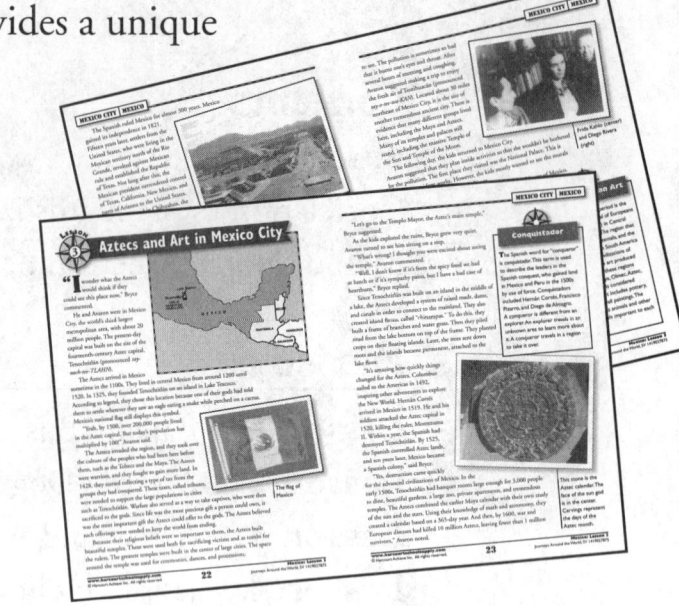

- Activities reinforce social studies skills, including map skills, time lines, charts, and graphs.

- Activities reinforce key vocabulary.

- Comprehension questions are in standardized test format.

- Writing prompts provide practice in different writing modes.

- A multimedia research activity emphasizes Internet research.

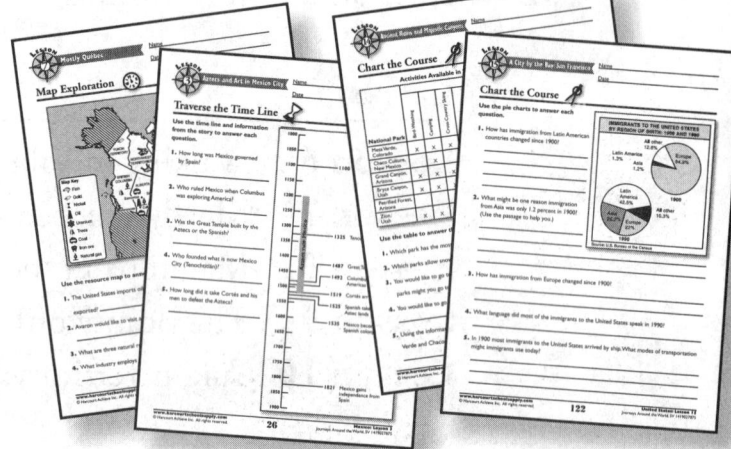

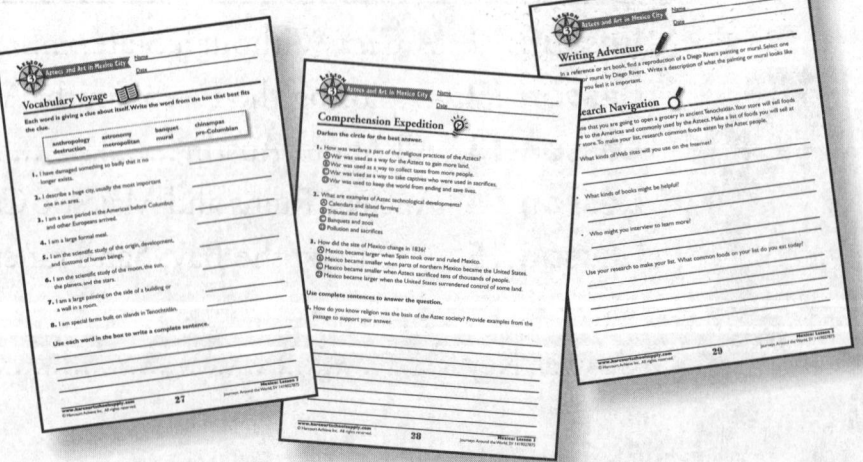

Correlation to Standards

Content Strands	Lessons
Culture	
Understands the similarities and differences within and among cultures in different societies	2, 3, 4, 5, 6, 7, 8, 9, 10, 14
Understands the relationship that exists between artistic, creative, and literary expressions and the societies that produce them	3, 4, 8, 9
Identifies institutions basic to all societies, including government, economic, educational, and religious institutions	3, 4, 5, 6, 9
Understands the relationships among religion, philosophy, and culture	1, 3, 4, 5, 9
Studies the roles of people in each society, including class structures, family life, warfare, religious beliefs and practices, and slavery	1, 3, 4, 5, 9
Describes the artistic and oral traditions and architecture in the three civilizations	1, 3, 4, 5, 8
Time, Continuity, and Change	
Understands historical chronology and the historical perspective	2–15
Explains how and where each empire arose and how the Aztec and Incan empires were defeated by the Spanish	1, 2, 3, 5
Describes what is known through archaeological studies of the early physical and cultural development of humankind from the Paleolithic era to the agricultural revolution	2, 3, 5, 6, 14
Understands how language, ideas, and institutions of one culture can influence other cultures (e.g., through trade, exploration, and immigration)	3, 5, 6, 7, 8, 9, 15
Understands the institution and impact of missionaries on Christianity and the diffusion of Christianity from Europe to other parts of the world in the medieval and early modern periods; locates missions on a world map	1, 4, 9, 15
Knows the major events that shaped the development of various cultures (e.g., the spread of agrarian societies, population movements, technological and cultural innovation, and the emergence of new population centers	1, 2, 3, 5, 6, 7, 8, 9, 10
Identifies reasons for European exploration and colonization of North America	3, 6, 7
Traces the civil rights and equal rights movements of various groups	12
Explains the major issues and events of the Mexican War and their impact on the United States	13, 14
Understands how individuals, events, and issues shaped the history of Texas from Reconstruction through the beginning of the 20th century	13
Identifies individuals, events, and issues during the Republic of Texas and early Texas statehood	13
Analyzes the causes of and events leading to Texas statehood	13
Describes the Texas War for Independence and the Mexican-American War, including territorial settlements, the aftermath of the wars, and the effects the wars had on the lives of Americans, including Mexican Americans today	13, 14
Analyzes U.S. foreign policy in the early Republic	14

Content Strands	Lessons
Describes the purpose, challenges, and economic incentives associated with westward expansion, including the concept of Manifest Destiny	14
Explains the political, economic, and social roots of Manifest Destiny	14
Analyzes the relationship between the concept of Manifest Destiny and the westward growth of the nation	14
Knows the factors involved in the development of cities and industries	15
People, Places, and Environments	
Understands the world in spatial terms	1–15
Understands the interactions of people and the physical environment	3, 5, 6, 7, 9, 10, 14
Uses maps, globes, graphs, charts, models, and databases to answer geographic questions	1–15
Understands the characteristics and relative locations of major historical and contemporary societies	1, 2, 3, 4, 5, 7, 9, 10, 14
Understands how geographic factors influence the economic development, political relationships, and policies of societies	1, 2, 3, 4, 5, 6, 7, 8, 9, 10, 14
Studies the locations, landforms, and climates of Mexico, Central America, and South America and their effects on Mayan, Aztec, and Incan economies, trade, and development of urban societies	1, 2, 3, 5
Knows the changing boundaries of the United States and describes the relationships the country had with its neighbors (current Mexico and Canada) and Europe, including the influence of the Monroe Doctrine, and how those relationships influenced westward expansion and the Mexican-American War	2, 3, 13, 14
Identifies the locations of human communities that populated the major regions of the world and describes how humans adapted to a variety of environments	1, 2, 3, 5, 6, 7, 9, 10, 14
Traces the boundaries constituting the North and the South and the geographical differences between the two regions	12
Identifies areas that were acquired to form the United States	13, 14
Knows the causes and consequences of urbanization that occurred in the United States after 1880	12, 15
Analyzes the divergent paths of the American people in the West from 1800 to the mid-1800s and the challenges they faced	14, 15
Examines the location and effects of urbanization, renewed immigration, and industrialization	15
Understands the role of physical and cultural geography in shaping events in the United States since 1880 (e.g., western settlement, immigration patterns, and urbanization)	15
Individual Development and Identity	
Understands how scarcity requires individuals and institutions to make choices about how to use resources	6, 10, 14

www.harcourtschoolsupply.com
© Harcourt Achieve Inc. All rights reserved.

Correlation to Standards
Journeys Around the World, SV 1419027875

Correlation to Standards

Content Strands	Lessons
Individuals, Groups, and Institutions	
Describes the Meso-American achievements in astronomy and mathematics, including the development of the calendar and the Meso-American knowledge of seasonal changes to the civilizations' agricultural systems	3, 5
Understands the contributions of individuals and groups from various cultures to selected historical and contemporary societies	2, 3, 8, 9, 14
Analyzes the contributions of people of various racial, ethnic, and religious groups to our national identity	12, 14
Identifies the political, social, and economic contributions of women to American society	12
Identifies the contributions of significant individuals including Stephen F. Austin	12
Explains the roles played by significant individuals during the Texas Revolution, including Sam Houston	12
Identifies selected racial, ethnic, and religious groups that settled in the United States and their reasons for immigration	15
Power, Authority, and Governance	
Understands alternative ways of organizing governments	1, 3, 6
Describes the basic lawmaking process and how the Constitution provides numerous opportunities for citizens to participate in the political process and to monitor and influence government (e.g., function of elections, political parties, interest groups)	11
Describes the principles of federalism, dual sovereignty, separation of powers, checks and balances, the nature and purpose of majority rule, and the ways in which the American idea of constitutionalism preserves individual rights	11
Analyzes how the U.S. Constitution reflects the principles of limited government, republicanism, checks and balances, federalism, separation of powers, popular sovereignty, and individual rights	11
Enumerates the powers of government set forth in the Constitution and the fundamental liberties ensured by the Bill of Rights	11
Summarizes the rights guaranteed in the Bill of Rights	11
Understands traditional historical points of reference in U.S. history through 1877	11, 12
Understands the impact of landmark Supreme Court cases	12
Production, Distribution, and Consumption	
Discusses the exchanges of plants, animals, technology, culture, and ideas among Europe, Africa, Asia, and the Americas in the fifteenth and sixteenth centuries and the major economic and social effects on each continent	3, 6, 7, 8, 13

Content Strands	Lessons
Traces patterns of agricultural and industrial development as they relate to climate, use of natural resources, markets, and trade, and locates such development on a map	9, 10, 12
Analyzes how physical characteristics of the environment influenced population distribution, settlement patterns, and economic activities in the United States during the eighteenth and nineteenth centuries	12, 14
Science, Technology, and Society	
Discusses the climatic changes and human modifications of the physical environment that gave rise to the domestication of plants and animals and new sources of clothing and shelter	3, 6, 8, 10
Understands the impact of interactions between people and the physical environment on the development of places and regions	3, 4, 5, 6, 7, 8, 9, 10, 14
Analyzes the impact of transportation systems on the growth, development, and urbanization of the United States	15
Global Connections	
Understands how language, ideas, and institutions of one culture can influence other cultures (e.g., through trade, exploration, and immigration)	2, 6, 7, 8, 9, 10, 15
Identifies the new sources of large-scale immigration and the contributions of immigrants to the building of cities and the economy; explains the ways in which new social and economic patterns encouraged assimilation of newcomers into the mainstream amid growing cultural diversity	8, 9, 10, 15
Civil Ideas and Practices	
Understands that the nature of citizenship varies among societies	7
Understands the relationship among individual rights, responsibilities, and freedoms in democratic societies	12
Understands the rights and responsibilities of citizens of the United States	12
Identifies reasons for and the impact of selected examples of civil disobedience in U.S. history	12
Analyzes the contributions of Texas leaders such as Barbara Jordan	13
Social Studies Skills	
Applies critical-thinking skills to organize and use information acquired from a variety of sources, including electronic technology	1–15
Organizes and interprets information from outlines, reports, databases, and visuals, including graphs, charts, time lines, and maps	1–15
Communicates in written, oral, and visual forms	1–15

Map of North America

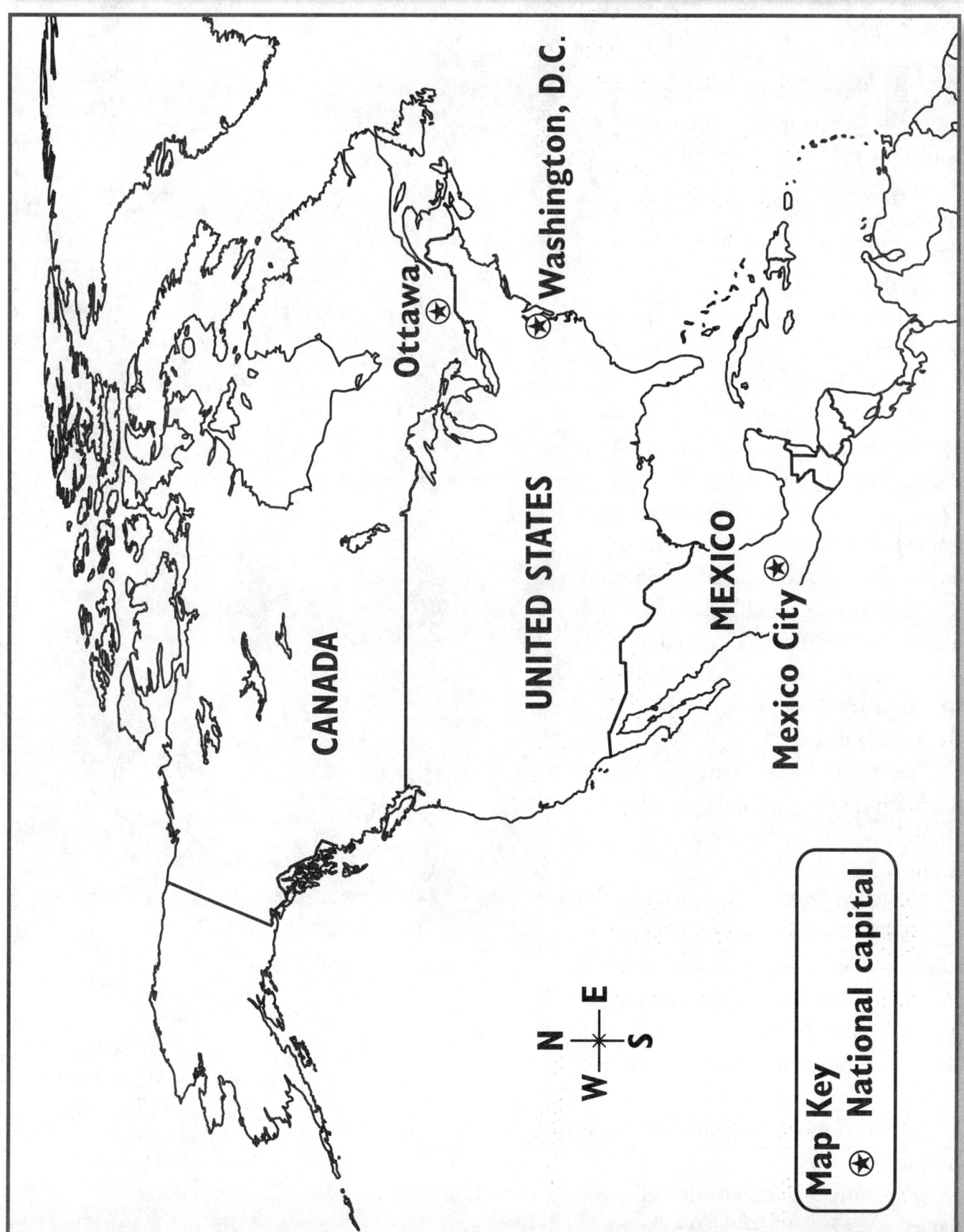

LESSON 1: Baja by Bus

"Tijuana is known as the world's most visited border town. With a population of about two million people, it is also one of Mexico's largest cities," Avaron noted.

"Yeah, and it's got a freaky wax museum, so let's hurry up and find it," Bryce replied.

The kids found the museum, populated with figures from Mexican history as well as Elvis Presley, Whoopi Goldberg, Bill Clinton, and Jack the Ripper. What Bryce most wanted to see, however, was an Aztec display that showed a human sacrifice.

"The Aztecs gave offerings of humans so that their gods would protect and help them. The ceremonies were held at the top of a pyramid," Bryce explained.

"Yes, but didn't the Aztecs live in the south-central part of the country, around present-day Mexico City?" Avaron asked.

"Well, that was the center of their civilization. However, by the 1400s, they ruled most of Mexico," Bryce replied. "And even though they didn't settle in Baja, I couldn't resist seeing this display after reading about it in my guidebook."

After touring the museum, the kids went to a restaurant for lunch.

"Do you know what tomatoes, vanilla, and chocolate have in common?" Avaron asked.

"I'm going to guess that they all originally came from Mexico," Bryce replied.

Traffic backs up at the border crossing from San Diego, California, into Tijuana, Mexico.

"You're right. And any country that creates chocolate is all right with me," laughed Avaron.

Their next stop was Mexitlán Theme Park. This cultural theme park has about 200 detailed scale models of Mexico's main attractions, including the Mayan ruins of Chichén Itzá and Palenque.

"We could learn everything we need to know about Mexico by just studying these models," Bryce commented.

"That would be a little bit like visitors to Las Vegas saying they experience French culture just because there's a statue of the Eiffel Tower there," Avaron replied.

"Oh, I know. I was only kidding. But this is pretty cool," Bryce said.

Located in northwestern Mexico, Baja is the world's third-longest peninsula. About 800 miles long, it is made up of two states, Baja California and Baja California Sur (*sur* means "south"). The Sea of Cortez, also known as the Gulf of California, is on the east side, the Pacific Ocean lies to the west, and a mountain range runs lengthwise through the peninsula.

The Vizcaino Desert is located near the center of Baja. The peninsula's climate is warm and dry, and its interior is mostly undeveloped. It has the fewest people of any Mexican state. It also boasts over 2,000 miles of coastline, including many spectacular white sand beaches.

"Hey, our bus leaves in half an hour. We'd better go to the station now," Bryce said.

The kids planned to travel through Baja by bus on Highway 1. Finished in 1973, this road allowed people to drive the length of the peninsula for the first time. Most of the highway is only two lanes wide. Measuring 1,059 miles, it is still the only road that covers the length of the peninsula.

As the bus traveled along the western coast, it passed through Ensenada, Baja's leading seaport. Ensenada also marked the end of the four-lane highway. Hours later, the kids got off the bus in El Rosario.

"Just think, this used to be the end of the road. And the bus from Ensenada only traveled to El Rosario once a week. I sure am glad they built Highway 1," Avaron said.

They ordered dinner from a taco stand and found a room at a small motel.

The next morning, they caught another bus. It was slowed by the steep climbs because the road begins crossing the mountains here. The bus was also slowed by numerous potholes and herds of livestock wandering across the highway. Another hazard was the steep cliffs with no guardrails.

Political Divisions

Mexico is divided into 31 states and one federal district. Similar to the states in the United States, each state in Mexico has its own constitution and a governor who is elected by the citizens. The capital, Mexico City, is located in the federal district, which is a special political division.

BAJA | MEXICO

"Maybe we should have just stayed on the bus last night," Avaron said.

"Why?" asked Bryce.

"Because I'd prefer to not see all of the scary drop-offs," Avaron answered.

The landscape was filled with a variety of cactus, as well as numerous cirio trees. These odd trees grow 50 feet high. They have wide bases and thin tops. They got their name because *cirio* is Spanish for "candle," which is what they look like. Their trunks are covered with tiny, thin branches, covered with leaves. On old trees, the trunk splits into two branches.

The bus banged and bounced onward to Guerrero Negro. This town supports itself by harvesting salt. Water is directed from the ocean into shallow ponds. Here the water evaporates, leaving behind a layer of sea salt. More than six million tons of salt are produced each year, making Guerrero Negro the world's largest salt production facility.

After a good night's rest, the kids were excited about their next adventure.

"Are you ready for the whale-watching tour?" Bryce asked.

"You'd better believe it. And I sure will be glad to trade the bus for a boat for a few hours," Avaron replied.

The cirio tree is also called a boojum tree.

California gray whales migrate from Canada and Alaska all the way down to Mexico each winter. The round-trip journey is close to 10,000 miles, making it one of the longest migrations of any animal. The whales arrive in December and January and usually stay until April, enjoying the warm waters of the lagoons. Lagoons are shallow channels that are connected to larger bodies of water.

The kids joined other tourists in a *panga*, which is a small Mexican fishing boat. After a thirty-minute ride, the tour guide slowed down and then pointed to a spout in the distance.

"That is coming from a whale's blowhole," he said.

Soon they saw a whale breach, or leap out of the water. Everyone in the boat cried out excitedly and snapped photos. Moments later, a mother whale and her baby approached the boat. The mother nudged the baby forward. Gray whales are curious and friendly. The baby stuck its head up next to the boat. Bryce and Avaron were sitting close by, and they both reached out to pat it.

"That was amazing," Avaron said. Bryce agreed, grinning for the entire return trip to shore.

The following day, the kids proceeded down Highway 1. They arrived in Mulege, on the eastern side of the peninsula. They were stunned by the beautiful clear blue water of the Sea of Cortez. They stayed for several days, recovering from their long bus trip, lying in the sun, swimming, and snorkeling.

Their next stop was La Paz, another city on the eastern coast. The Sea of Cortez receives more sunlight than any other sea on earth. Because the tides are so large, they churn up the nutrient-rich water from the bottom. As a result, the area is full of a vast variety of sea life. The kids saw dolphins, sea lions, giant manta rays, and lots of colorful fish.

Their final destination was Cabo San Lucas, located at the end of the peninsula. This major resort center has beautiful beaches. A Spanish mission was built here in 1730. It is still used today and is the most widely attended church in the area. The kids also visited the natural rock formations that have been carved into odd shapes by the wind and the water. Perhaps the most famous one is Land's End Arch, which stands where the Sea of Cortez and the Pacific Ocean meet.

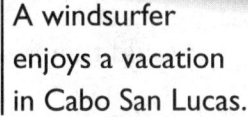

A windsurfer enjoys a vacation in Cabo San Lucas.

"A place named Land's End seems like a fitting place to end an exploration, don't you think?" Avaron asked.

"Yeah, and it's nice to be somewhere that is so beautiful and peaceful. Tomorrow we'll catch our flight out, unless you've decided you want to ride the bus back up to the top of the peninsula," Bryce said, grinning.

"Thanks for the offer, but I think a thousand miles by bus is enough for me. I'm ready for another mode of transportation," Avaron replied.

LESSON 1: Baja by Bus

Name _____

Date _____

Map Exploration

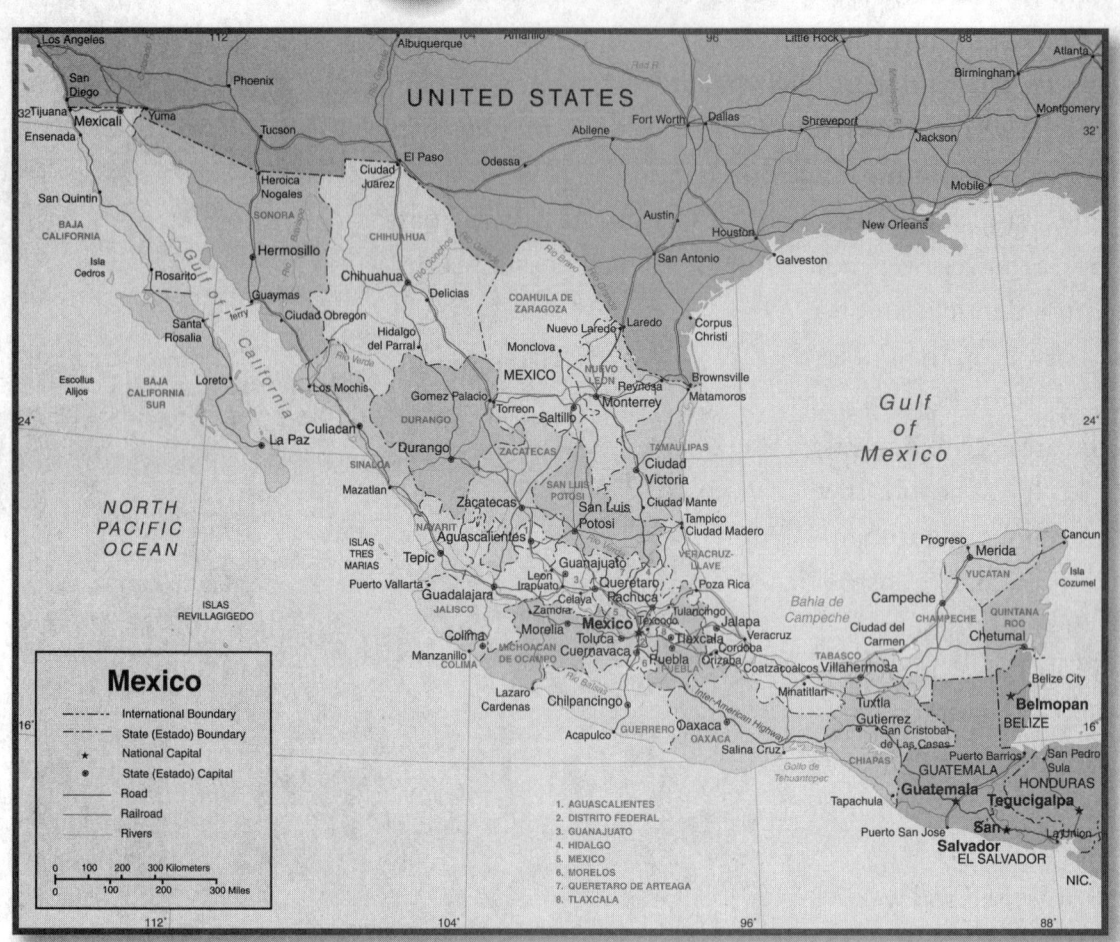

Use the map to answer the questions.

1. What body of water lies to the east of the Baja peninsula? _Gulf of Cal._

2. From what American city would people cross into Tijuana? _San Diego_

3. If Bryce and Avaron took a bus from Mexicali to Hermosillo, approximately how many miles would they travel? _325_

   Imagine there is a straight route between the two cities and the bus travels at a steady 60 miles per hour. How long would the bus trip take? _____

4. What city is found at approximately 24° latitude and 99° longitude? _Ciudad Victoria_

5. What body of water would you swim in at the beach in Tampico? _Bay of Campeche_

Name _____

Date _____

Vocabulary Voyage

Write the word from the box that matches the definition. Then use the numbered letters to complete the sentences to learn some facts about Mexico.

civilization	~~constitution~~	evaporate	~~lengthwise~~
~~migrate~~	~~lagoon~~	~~peninsula~~	~~pyramid~~

1. in the direction of the length   l e n g t h w i s e
                                       12 7   1

2. the way of life of people in a society   c i v i l i z a t i o n
                                              5   18   4

3. a massive building with a square base and four triangular sides   p y r a m i d
                                                                       2 3

4. the basic beliefs and laws of a country   c o n s t i t u t i o n
                                                 6   15

5. to move from one region to another on a regular schedule   m i g r a t e
                                                               17   14

6. a piece of land sticking out into a body of water   p e n i n s u l a
                                                        8   10 13

7. a shallow body of water connected with a sea   l a g o o n
                                                  19   11

8. change from a liquid state to a vapor   e v a p o r a t e
                                           9   20 16

Facts About Mexico:

The official language is   S p a n i s h .
                            1 2 3 4 5 6 7

The currency is the   p e s o .
                      8 9 10 11

Mexico is bordered by the United States, Belize, and   G u a t e m a l a .
                                                       12 13 14 15 16 17 18 19 20

Name _____

Date _____

Comprehension Expedition

Darken the circle for the best answer.

1. What might be a reason the interior of Baja is mostly undeveloped?
   Ⓐ It is used for resorts.
   Ⓑ It is a mountainous desert area.
   Ⓒ It can only be reached by bus.
   Ⓓ It only has one highway.

2. How do you know there was Spanish exploration in the Baja area of Mexico?
   Ⓐ It has spectacular beaches.
   Ⓑ A road runs the length of the peninsula.
   Ⓒ Aztecs once ruled the region.
   Ⓓ A mission is at the end of the peninsula.

3. How are the Mexican political divisions similar to those in the United States?
   Ⓐ Each state in Mexico is headed by a governor.
   Ⓑ The capital was once the center of a civilization.
   Ⓒ Large cities are found along the border.
   Ⓓ Each country has the same number of states.

Use complete sentences to answer the question.

4. Why might the production of salt help the Mexican economy?

_____
_____
_____
_____
_____
_____
_____

Name _____

Date _____

Writing Adventure

Imagine that you were a visitor to the Baja peninsula in 1965 before Highway 1 was built. How would you explore the peninsula? Keep in mind what you know about the geography of the area. Write a short story describing your trip.

Research Navigation

Use the U.S. Department of State Web site to answer the questions below.

http://travel.state.gov/travel/cis_pa_tw/cis/cis_2139.html

1. What documents do you need to enter Mexico?
_____
_____
_____

2. Do U.S. citizens need a visa to travel in Mexico?
_____
_____
_____

3. Is it safe to drink the water in Mexico?
_____
_____
_____

4. What should a driver know when taking a car to Mexico City?
_____
_____
_____

LESSON 2: A Little Dog and a Big State

"OK, where are all the little dogs?" Bryce asked.

"I don't know what you're talking about," Avaron replied.

"I'm talking about Chihuahuas, the smallest breed of dog. We're in the state of Chihuahua (pronounced *chee-WA-wa*) now, so where are all the dogs?" Bryce said, grinning.

"You're such a jokester," Avaron replied.

"Actually, I did some research on Chihuahuas. The earliest version of the breed was a dog that the Toltecs raised. The tiny dogs became popular after they were discovered in the state of Chihuahua in the 1850s and introduced to the world," said Bryce.

"And I did some research on the large state that these tiny dogs were named for. Chihuahua is Mexico's biggest state. It shares a border with Texas and New Mexico, and it is a large mineral producer," Avaron said.

The kids planned to spend one night in the capital, also named Chihuahua, before riding the train to Copper Canyon. They went to the Museum of the Revolution, housed in what was once Pancho Villa's 50-room mansion.

Pancho Villa (pronounced *VEE-yah*) has been described as a folk hero, a revolutionary, and a bandit. During the Mexican Revolution, he helped to overthrow the government and end a 30-year dictatorship. He was born in 1877 and was assassinated by a group of unknown men in 1923.

In 1916, he crossed the border into New Mexico and killed several American citizens. He was angry that the United States was supporting one of his fellow revolutionaries as the leader of Mexico. President Woodrow Wilson sent 10,000 American soldiers into Mexico to capture Villa. Despite searching for 11 months, they never found him.

"I read that Pancho Villa worked on the Copper Canyon railroad," Avaron noted.

The Toltecs

The Toltecs formed an empire in central Mexico during the tenth century and ruled until the twelfth century. They were skilled builders and craftspeople, and their culture emphasized a strong military. They used their strength to dominate other groups of people. This influenced later cultures, especially the Aztecs.

CHIHUAHUA | MEXICO

"I'm looking forward to our train trip. The railroad is a great feat of engineering. Its lowest point is sea level, and its highest is over 8,000 feet. At one point, the track does a 360-degree loop over itself!" said Bryce.

The Copper Canyon Railroad, whose official name is *Chihuahua al Pacífico*, has more than 30 major bridges and more than 80 tunnels. It covers 400 miles in a 13-hour trip.

The Copper Canyon is located in the southwestern part of the state. It is actually 6 interconnected massive canyons made up of 200 gorges instead of just 1 canyon. The canyon system is 4 times larger than the Grand Canyon, and 4 of its 6 canyons are deeper than the Grand Canyon.

The city of Chihuahua

The following morning, Bryce and Avaron boarded the train. After traveling 150 miles, they got off in Creel, a small town situated at an elevation of 7,669 feet. They bought some of the crafts the Tarahumara (pronounced *ta-ra-OO-ma-ra*) Indians were selling, including a small wooden ball like the ones used in the Indians' running game that covers extremely long distances.

Tarahumara is the Spanish name for these people, who call themselves *Raramuri*. The rough translation for *Raramuri* is "foot runners." While it is unknown how long these seminomadic people have moved around in this area, there is evidence of human habitation 3,000 years ago.

The Raramuri are expert farmers. They tend crops both on the high plateaus and in the canyon. Although they had contact with Jesuit missionaries in the 1600s and 1700s, the Raramuri defined Christianity in their own way, accepting practices and beliefs that had meaning for them and rejecting those that did not.

Avaron purchased a woven basket from a Raramuri girl. Bryce and Avaron were using their limited understanding of Spanish to communicate with the girl.

Avaron asked, "¿A usted le gusta correr?" (*Do you like to run?*) and the girl, whose name was Tiko, replied, "Sí, por supuesto." (*Yes, of course.*)

| CHIHUAHUA | MEXICO |

Then Tiko asked, "¿Usted desea competir?" (*Do you want to race?*)

Avaron grinned and nodded enthusiastically. She handed her backpack to Bryce, who indicated to Tiko that he would watch her crafts for her. The two girls walked out onto the street. Bryce waited until they were ready, and then he yelled, "¡Fuera!" (*Go!*)

Avaron and Tiko raced down the street. Avaron quickly realized they hadn't settled on an ending point. She and Tiko were side by side, and they were running too fast for Avaron to ask any questions. She needed to save her breath. So she just ran. They raced past the town plaza, a church, and many brightly painted buildings. They passed the train station, and then they passed a man riding a horse. Avaron was beginning to get tired. She tried to keep up with Tiko, but by the time they passed a second church, she was a step behind. The girls made a circle through town, and they raced past the plaza again. As they were approaching the first church they had run by, Avaron slowed down a little more. She could hear Bryce cheering from down the street, but she could not catch Tiko. Tiko looked back at her, smiled, passed Bryce, and then began the same route again. Avaron stopped by her brother, huffing and puffing, with her hands on her knees.

Tiko ran the entire loop again, and then stopped by Avaron, who was still breathing hard. The girls laughed, and Bryce went into a nearby shop and came back with three soft drinks. The children talked a little longer, until it was time for Bryce and Avaron to catch their ride into Copper Canyon.

The Raramuri are expert runners. In the past, they hunted by running alongside game until the animals were exhausted. They play multi-hour games involving kicking a small wooden ball. In recent years, some have participated in long-distance races such as the Leadville 100 in Colorado. This race is considered by many to be among the toughest long-distance races. Most of the

Although the area is called Copper Canyon, little copper was mined here. The name is due to the copper- and green-colored lichen that covers the canyon walls.

CHIHUAHUA | MEXICO

100-mile race takes place at elevations over 10,000 feet. The Raramuri who run these races frequently win or finish among the top ten. And they usually run in sandals made of old tires and leather thongs.

After saying good-bye to their new friend Tiko, Avaron and Bryce took an eight-hour trip down the bumpy one-lane road into the canyon. They traveled in an old school bus to the town of Batopilas. Located at the bottom of the canyon, this former silver-mining town was founded in 1709.

They found a room that looked out on the river. After a dinner of tacos and enchiladas served with fresh, handmade corn tortillas, the kids slept. The following day, they explored the Lost Mission. This church got its name because there are no records describing it. It is believed that it was built in the 1760s by Jesuits. Jesuits are a Roman Catholic order of religious men. These Spanish missionaries arrived in Copper Canyon in the early 1600s with the purpose of converting the people to Christianity.

After exploring the area around Batopilas for a couple of days, Bryce and Avaron returned to Creel, where they got back on the train and rode to Los Mochis, the end of the line. Los Mochis is about 15 miles east of the Sea of Cortez. The kids went for a boat ride in the bay, ate seafood, and then made the return trip to Chihuahua the following day.

As they strolled down the wide streets, Bryce stopped suddenly. He rummaged through his backpack, found his camera, and then ran down a narrow alley.

Moments later, he returned with a big grin on his face.

"I just took a picture of two very small dogs, in the capital of the largest Mexican state. I'm going to call it "Chihuahua, Chihuahua in Chihuahua, Chihuahua," he said, laughing, as Avaron rolled her eyes.

Popular Mexican dishes include chilis, beans, and tortillas.

Tortillas

A tortilla is a type of Mexican bread that is round, thin, and flat. It is usually made with cornmeal, although sometimes wheat flour is used. To make tacos, tortillas are folded around ingredients such as meat, beans, and cheese. To make enchiladas, tortillas are rolled around a filling and covered with sauce.

LESSON 2: A Little Dog and a Big State

Name _____

Date _____

Chart the Course

Use the table to answer each question.

1. Which state is the largest in size?
   Chihuahua

2. If you were to take this information and make a chart that ranked the states by population, which state would be first on your chart?
   Mexico

3. The density of a place is the average number of individuals in a unit of area. In this chart that unit of area is a square kilometer. The density numbers show the number of people per one square kilometer.

   What area is the most crowded?
   Federal District

4. Which state is larger in size, Baja California or (Baja California Sur?)
   _____

   Which of those two states has the denser population?
   Baja California

5. Which U.S. state is closest in size to Chihuahua?
   Oregon

Area and Population in Mexico

State	Area (square kilometers)	Population	Density
Aguascalientes	5,589	1,023,800	183.2
Baja California	70,113	2,846,500	40.6
Baja California Sur	73,677	477,200	6.5
Campeche	51,833	720,900	13.9
Chiapas	73,887	4,329,700	58.6
Chihuahua	247,087	3,274,700	13.3
Coahuila	151,571	2,395,100	15.8
Colima	5,455	581,100	106.5
Durango	119,648	1,449,100	12.1
Federal District (Distrito Federal)	1,499	8,720,700	5,817.7
Guanajuato	30,589	4,919,000	160.8
Guerrero	63,749	3,196,100	50.1
Hidalgo	20,987	2,330,900	111.1
Jalisco	80,137	6,540,700	81.6
México	21,461	14,349,700	668.6
Michoacán	59,864	4,066,900	67.9
Morelos	4,941	1,637,400	331.4
Nayarit	27,621	942,200	34.1
Nuevo León	64,555	4,041,300	62.6
Oaxaca	95,364	3,651,100	38.3
Puebla	33,919	5,480,200	161.6
Querétaro	11,769	1,558,500	132.4
Quintana Roo	50,350	1,023,500	20.3
San Luis Potosí	62,848	2,370,400	37.7
Sinaloa	58,092	2,574,300	44.3
Sonora	184,934	2,262,700	12.2
Tabasco	24,661	1,994,700	80.9
Tamaulipas	79,829	2,927,300	36.7
Tlaxcala	3,914	1,034,600	264.3
Veracruz	72,815	6,980,900	95.9
Yucatán	39,340	1,714,100	43.6
Zacatecas	75,040	1,381,900	18.4

Area of Selected U.S. States

U.S. State	Area (square kilometers)
California	403,934
Florida	139,671
Nevada	284,449
New York	122,284
Oregon	248,632

Vocabulary Voyage

Write the word from the box to complete each set of related words.

| converting | elevation | gorge |
| habitation | missionary | nomad |

1. traveler, wanderer, _____

2. preacher, minister, _____

3. dwelling, home, _____

4. ravine, canyon, _____

5. transforming, changing, _____

6. height, distance, _____

Use each word in the box to write a complete sentence.

_____
_____
_____
_____
_____
_____
_____
_____

Name _____
Date _____

Comprehension Expedition

Darken the circle for the best answer.

1. Why is Pancho Villa important to Mexico's history?
   Ⓐ He was born in Durango and lived in Chihuahua.
   Ⓑ He was never captured by American military forces.
   Ⓒ He was assassinated on his ranch in 1923.
   Ⓓ He helped lead a revolution against an oppressive dictator.

2. What is the most likely reason the Raramuri are sometimes nomadic?
   Ⓐ They travel so they can farm year-round.
   Ⓑ They travel to run in long races.
   Ⓒ They travel to buy footwear.
   Ⓓ They travel to a large canyon.

3. What is one likely reason the Raramuri developed multi-hour running games?
   Ⓐ To practice for hunting
   Ⓑ To become expert farmers
   Ⓒ To win long-distance races
   Ⓓ To prepare for battle

Use complete sentences to answer the question.

4. How do you know that the Copper Canyon was not isolated from civilization? Give two examples.

_____
_____
_____
_____
_____
_____
_____

Name _____

Date _____

Writing Adventure

Write step-by-step directions about how to prepare a lunch that includes tortillas. You may wish to use information from the passage, recipes, interviews, or your own experience.

Research Navigation

It is important to know what kind of weather to expect when traveling to an area. Imagine you are planning a trip to the city of Chihuahua in Chihuahua, Mexico. Follow these steps to see what kind of weather you can expect.

1. Go to the Internet site below.

   www.weather.com

2. Enter city and country in the *Local Weather* box.

3. Click on *Month*.

4. Imagine your trip will be the last week of this month. Find the data for the last week of this month.

What kind of temperatures will you encounter? How will this information affect what you are taking on the trip? Will there be rain during your stay? (Precipitation, or rain or snow, is abbreviated *precip*.)

Aztecs and Art in Mexico City

"I wonder what the Aztecs would think if they could see this place now," Bryce commented.

He and Avaron were in Mexico City, the world's third-largest metropolitan area, with about 20 million people. The present-day capital was built on the site of the fourteenth-century Aztec capital, Tenochtitlán (pronounced *tay-noch-tee-TLAHN*).

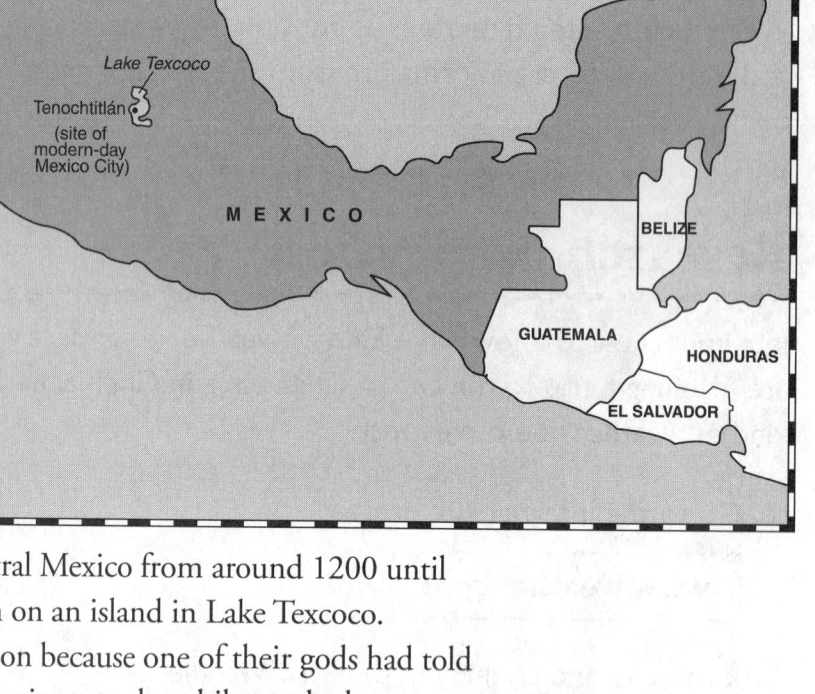

The Aztecs arrived in Mexico sometime in the 1100s. They lived in central Mexico from around 1200 until 1520. In 1325, they founded Tenochtitlán on an island in Lake Texcoco. According to legend, they chose this location because one of their gods had told them to settle wherever they saw an eagle eating a snake while perched on a cactus. Mexico's national flag still displays this symbol.

"Yeah, by 1500, over 200,000 people lived in the Aztec capital. But today's population has multiplied by 100!" Avaron said.

The Aztecs invaded the region, and they took over the culture of the peoples who had been here before them, such as the Toltecs and the Maya. The Aztecs were warriors, and they fought to gain more land. In 1428, they started collecting a type of tax from the groups they had conquered. These taxes, called tributes, were needed to support the large populations in cities such as Tenochtitlán. Warfare also served as a way to take captives, who were then sacrificed to the gods. Since life was the most precious gift a person could own, it was the most important gift the Aztecs could offer to the gods. The Aztecs believed such offerings were needed to keep the world from ending.

The flag of Mexico

Because their religious beliefs were so important to them, the Aztecs built beautiful temples. These were used both for sacrificing victims and as tombs for the rulers. The greatest temples were built in the center of large cities. The space around the temple was used for ceremonies, dances, and processions.

"Let's go to the Templo Mayor, the Aztec's main temple," Bryce suggested.

As the kids explored the ruins, Bryce grew very quiet. Avaron turned to see him sitting on a step.

"What's wrong? I thought you were excited about seeing the temple," Avaron commented.

"Well, I don't know if it's from the spicy food we had at lunch or if it's sympathy pains, but I have a bad case of heartburn," Bryce replied.

Since Tenochtitlán was built on an island in the middle of a lake, the Aztecs developed a system of raised roads, dams, and canals in order to connect to the mainland. They also created island farms, called "chinampas." To do this, they built a frame of branches and water grass. Then they piled mud from the lake bottom on top of the frame. They planted crops on these floating islands. Later, the trees sent down roots and the islands became permanent, attached to the lake floor.

"It's amazing how quickly things changed for the Aztecs. Columbus sailed to the Americas in 1492, inspiring other adventurers to explore the New World. Hernán Cortés arrived in Mexico in 1519. He and his soldiers attacked the Aztec capital in 1520, killing the ruler, Montezuma II. Within a year, the Spanish had destroyed Tenochtitlán. By 1525, the Spanish controlled Aztec lands, and ten years later, Mexico became a Spanish colony," said Bryce.

"Yes, destruction came quickly for the advanced civilizations of Mexico. In the early 1500s, Tenochtitlán had banquet rooms large enough for 3,000 people to dine, beautiful gardens, a large zoo, private apartments, and tremendous temples. The Aztecs combined the earlier Maya calendar with their own study of the sun and the stars. Using their knowledge of math and astronomy, they created a calendar based on a 365-day year. And then, by 1600, war and European diseases had killed 10 million Aztecs, leaving fewer than 1 million survivors," Avaron noted.

Conquistador

The Spanish word for "conqueror" is *conquistador*. This term is used to describe the leaders in the Spanish conquest, who gained land in Mexico and Peru in the 1500s by use of force. Conquistadors included Hernán Cortés, Francisco Pizarro, and Diego de Almagro. A conqueror is different from an explorer. An explorer travels in an unknown area to learn more about it. A conqueror travels in a region to take it over.

This stone is the Aztec calendar. The face of the sun god is in the center. Carvings represent the days of the Aztec month.

MEXICO CITY | MEXICO

The Spanish ruled Mexico for almost 300 years. Mexico gained its independence in 1821. Fifteen years later, settlers from the United States, who were living in the Mexican territory north of the Rio Grande, revolted against Mexican rule and established the Republic of Texas. Not long after this, the Mexican president surrendered control of Texas, California, New Mexico, and parts of Arizona to the United States.

"As we learned in Chihuahua, the Mexican Revolution occurred in 1910. It ended in the 1930s, and at this time, socialist values became national policy. The Revolutionary Party ruled until 2000. Today's government is similar to the U.S. government. It is a federal republic, and its president is elected to a 6-year term," Avaron noted.

The kids' next stop was the National Anthropology Museum. This tremendous place is considered one of the top museums in the world. It contains information about the origin, development, and customs of the peoples who lived in Mexico. The museum displays artifacts from all of the civilizations that existed in Mexico before the arrival of the Spanish.

Mexico City is partially surrounded by mountains and towering volcanoes. However, because it is so large and so heavily polluted, they can be difficult

Mexico is home to many ancient pyramids, including the Pyramid of the Sun and Pyramid of the Moon in Teotihuacán.

The National Palace in Mexico City

to see. The pollution is sometimes so bad that it burns one's eyes and throat. After several hours of sneezing and coughing, Avaron suggested making a trip to enjoy the fresh air of Teotihuacán (pronounced *tay-o-tee-wa-KAN*). Located about 30 miles northeast of Mexico City, it is the site of another tremendous ancient city. There is evidence that many different groups lived here, including the Maya and Aztecs. Many of its temples and palaces still stand, including the massive Temple of the Sun and Temple of the Moon.

Frida Kahlo (center) and Diego Rivera (right)

The following day, the kids returned to Mexico City. Avaron suggested that they plan inside activities so that she wouldn't be bothered by the pollution. The first place they visited was the National Palace. This is where the president works. However, the kids mostly wanted to see the murals painted by the famous artist Diego Rivera.

These murals, or paintings applied to a wall, show the history of Mexico. Although Rivera worked on them for 25 years, he died before he finished.

"I don't always understand Rivera's murals, but I can appreciate his importance as an artist," Bryce said. "He wanted to take his art to the public by painting it on streets and buildings. His paintings depict historical and political events in a realist style."

"I think our next stop should be the Frida Kahlo Museum," said Avaron.

"Yes, that's fitting, since she and Rivera were married," Bryce replied.

Located in the house where she was born and where she and Rivera lived for 25 years, the Frida Kahlo Museum is filled with her art, as well as with the many things they collected together. Both were interested in pre-Columbian art. Kahlo's paintings often reflected events in her personal life. She is known for her self-portraits, paintings she made of herself.

"Both Diego Rivera and Frida Kahlo made beautiful and important art known the world over," Avaron commented.

Pre-Columbian Art

The pre-Columbian period is the time before the arrival of Europeans (Columbus and after) in Central and South America. The region that is now Mexico, Guatemala, and the Andes Mountains in South America was occupied by civilizations of native peoples. The art produced by the peoples of these regions (including the Maya, Olmec, Aztec, Toltec, and Inca) is considered pre-Columbian. It includes pottery, sculpture, and wall paintings. The art often depicts animals and other religious symbols important to each culture.

LESSON 3: Aztecs and Art in Mexico City

Name _____

Date _____

Traverse the Time Line

Use the time line and information from the story to answer each question.

1. How long was Mexico governed by Spain?
   _____

2. Who ruled Mexico when Columbus was exploring America?
   _____

3. Was the Great Temple built by the Aztecs or the Spanish?
   _____

4. Who founded what is now Mexico City (Tenochtitlán)?
   _____

5. How long did it take Cortés and his men to defeat the Aztecs?
   _____

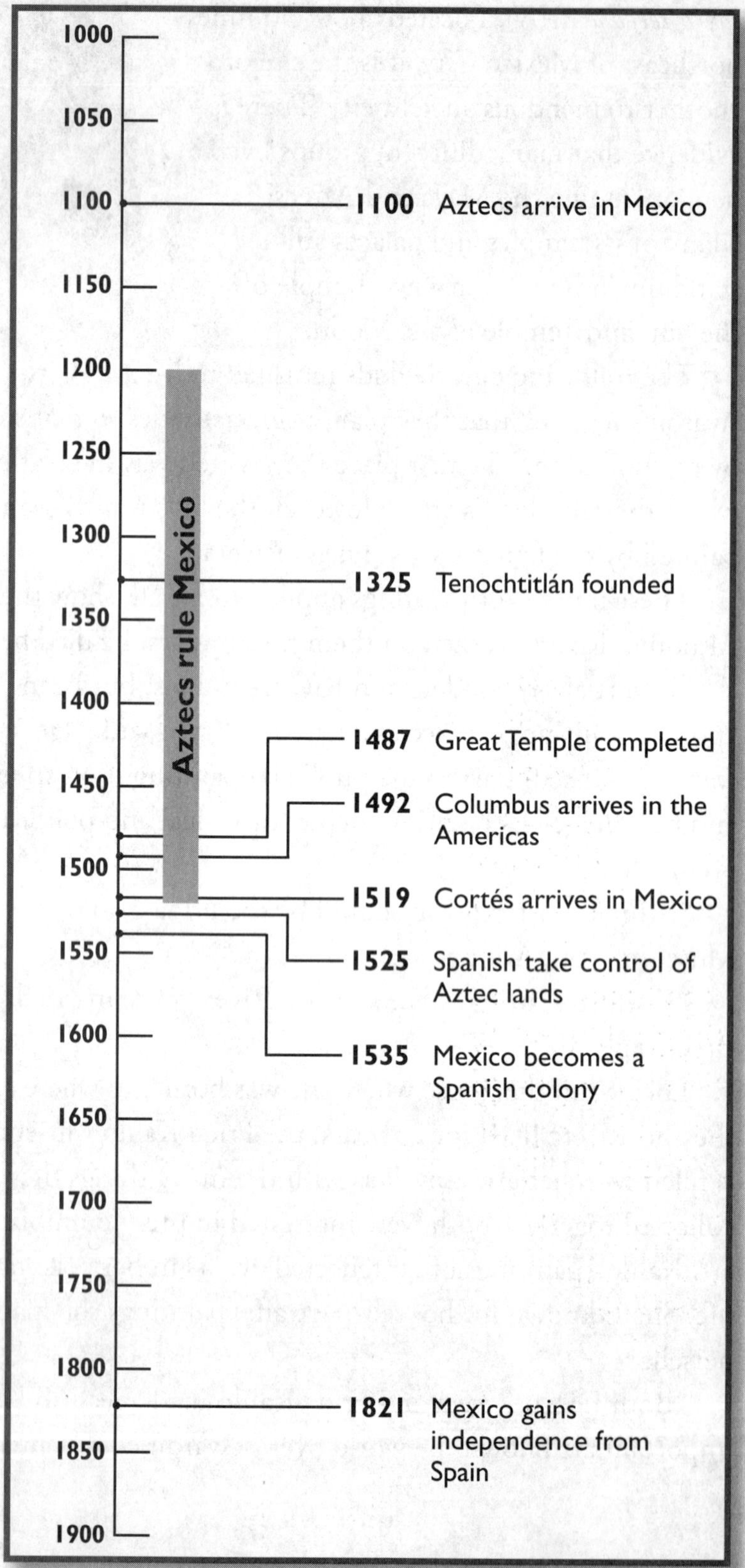

Time line:
- 1100 Aztecs arrive in Mexico
- Aztecs rule Mexico (1200–1520)
- 1325 Tenochtitlán founded
- 1487 Great Temple completed
- 1492 Columbus arrives in the Americas
- 1519 Cortés arrives in Mexico
- 1525 Spanish take control of Aztec lands
- 1535 Mexico becomes a Spanish colony
- 1821 Mexico gains independence from Spain

www.harcourtschoolsupply.com
© Harcourt Achieve Inc. All rights reserved.

26

Mexico: Lesson 3
Journeys Around the World, SV 1419027875

Vocabulary Voyage

Each word is giving a clue about itself. Write the word from the box that best fits the clue.

| anthropology | astronomy | banquet | chinampas |
| destruction | metropolitan | mural | pre-Columbian |

1. I have damaged something so badly that it no longer exists. _____

2. I describe a huge city, usually the most important one in an area. _____

3. I am a time period in the Americas before Columbus and other Europeans arrived. _____

4. I am a large formal meal. _____

5. I am the scientific study of the origin, development, and customs of human beings. _____

6. I am the scientific study of the moon, the sun, the planets, and the stars. _____

7. I am a large painting on the side of a building or a wall in a room. _____

8. I am special farms built on islands in Tenochtitlán. _____

Use each word in the box to write a complete sentence.

_____
_____
_____
_____

Name _____

Date _____

Comprehension Expedition

Darken the circle for the best answer.

1. How was warfare a part of the religious practices of the Aztecs?
   Ⓐ War was used as a way for the Aztecs to gain more land.
   Ⓑ War was used as a way to collect taxes from more people.
   Ⓒ War was used as a way to take captives who were used in sacrifices.
   Ⓓ War was used to keep the world from ending and save lives.

2. What are examples of Aztec technological developments?
   Ⓐ Calendars and island farming
   Ⓑ Tributes and temples
   Ⓒ Banquets and zoos
   Ⓓ Pollution and sacrifices

3. How did the size of Mexico change in 1836?
   Ⓐ Mexico became larger when Spain took over and ruled Mexico.
   Ⓑ Mexico became smaller when parts of northern Mexico became the United States.
   Ⓒ Mexico became smaller when Aztecs sacrificed tens of thousands of people.
   Ⓓ Mexico became larger when the United States surrendered control of some land.

Use complete sentences to answer the question.

4. How do you know religion was the basis of the Aztec society? Provide examples from the passage to support your answer.

_____
_____
_____
_____
_____
_____
_____
_____

LESSON 3: Aztecs and Art in Mexico City

Name _____
Date _____

Writing Adventure

In a reference or art book, find a reproduction of a Diego Rivera painting or mural. Select one painting or mural by Diego Rivera. Write a description of what the painting or mural looks like and why you feel it is important.

Research Navigation

Imagine that you are going to open a grocery in ancient Tenochtitlán. Your store will sell foods native to the Americas and commonly used by the Aztecs. Make a list of foods you will sell at your store. To make your list, research common foods eaten by the Aztec people.

- What kinds of Web sites will you use on the Internet?
  _____
  _____

- What kinds of books might be helpful?
  _____
  _____

- Who might you interview to learn more?
  _____
  _____

Use your research to make your list. What common foods on your list do you eat today?
_____
_____
_____
_____

Lesson 4: Jalisco Holiday

The first thing Avaron wanted to do after arriving in Guadalajara (pronounced *gwah-dah-lah-HAH-rah*), the capital of Jalisco (pronounced *hall-EES-koh*), was hear some mariachi music. Mariachi (pronounced *ma-ree-AH-chee*) is a Mexican orchestra. There are usually between three and twelve musicians, playing guitars, violins, and trumpets.

"Mariachi began in Jalisco. I'm guessing we might hear some music if we go to the Plaza de los Mariachis. What do you think?" said Avaron.

The kids went to the plaza, located in the town's Historic Center, and listened to the musicians. The musicians were dressed in the costume of the charro, or cowboy. They wore short jackets, pants with buttons down the side of the leg, western boots, and sombreros, or wide-brimmed straw hats. Avaron could not sit still, as the lively beat of the music made her clap her hands and tap her feet. Nearby, several people danced and swayed. After hearing several songs, Bryce was ready to move on. The kids walked to the Metropolitan Cathedral.

Construction on the large church started around 1558 and ended around 1616. It has twin towers and many elaborate altars. It is surrounded by four plazas, or public squares. The plazas were full of food stalls, vendors, and musicians.

Bryce and Avaron next visited the Government Palace. Home to the state government offices, the building also contains two of José Clemente Orozco's murals. One of the paintings shows Father Miguel Hidalgo, the priest who is

A cathedral is a large church that serves as the main church in a district. The Cathedral sits in the center of the historic district and is a good starting point for a walking tour of central Guadalajara.

known as the father of Mexican Independence. Hidalgo rang his church's bell in order to announce the revolution against the Spanish on September 16, 1810. The date is now celebrated as Mexico's Independence Day, even though it would be another 11 years before the country was free of Spanish rule.

"José Clemente Orozco was the most famous mural painter of the twentieth century. He was studying architecture when he lost his left hand in an accident. This helped him decide to pursue art," said Avaron.

"And his work helped Mexican art to gain an international audience," Bryce noted.

The kids went to the plaza just north of the cathedral to see the Rotunda de los Hombres Ilustres. This monument has twelve bronze sculptures of twelve famous men from Jalisco. Six of them are buried under the Rotunda.

"I'm getting hungry," Bryce said.

"Well, there's no shortage of restaurants to choose from. Do you want to try that one?" Avaron asked, pointing across the street.

The kids enjoyed a delicious meal. Bryce had a whole barbecued fish stuffed with vegetables. Avaron had Mexico's national dish: a large mild chili stuffed with ground beef and topped with walnut sauce and pomegranate seeds. Its colors match those found on the Mexican flag (green chili, white sauce, red seeds). For dessert, they ordered flan, a popular sweet custard.

After eating, they hired a calandria. This small horse-drawn carriage carried them through the downtown area and then to the Libertad Market. This is one of the largest markets in Mexico under one roof. Three stories high, it contains clothing, meat and vegetable stalls, and crafts made of glass, leather, straw, tin, and wood.

"Look at these boots!" Avaron held up a pair of snakeskin boots with a snake head attached to each toe.

"I want to buy some huaraches," Bryce said.

He tried on a pair of the sturdy Mexican sandals. "These are perfect. I'm going to get them, unless you think I should buy the snakeskin boots instead," he said, grinning.

"Get the sandals," Avaron replied.

The dome-shaped ceiling in this church was painted by José Clemente Orozco. The circular painting in the center is called "The Man of Fire."

JALSICO | MEXICO

After buying the huaraches, the kids passed through another plaza. A couple was doing the Mexican hat dance, which originated in Guadalajara. The man was dressed like a charro, and the woman was wearing a colorful full skirt. They twirled around a sombrero that was lying on the ground.

The following morning, the kids traveled west to the Potrero Chico National Park. Full of dramatic limestone peaks, the park attracts rock climbers from all over the world. Avaron signed up for a daylong beginner's course.

"Hey, Bryce, are you sure you don't want to come with me?" she asked.

"Yeah, you can have the rattlesnakes, scorpions, and tarantulas all to yourself today. I'm going to catch up with my journal writing," Bryce replied.

Avaron's class went to Buzz Rock, where they learned how to put on their climbing harnesses, how to communicate while climbing, and other basic climbing and safety techniques. When it was Avaron's turn to scramble up the rock, her instructor told her she was a natural. Later that afternoon, Bryce joined Avaron and some of the other climbers for a relaxing soak in the hot springs.

The next day, the kids continued their journey west, traveling to the coastal city of Puerto Vallarta. They enjoyed the beautiful blue water while they sat on white sand beaches lined with palm trees. The Sierra Madre mountain range ran along the eastern horizon.

They toured the jungle by horseback in the afternoon, and then they went to the famous boardwalk. This walkway along the oceanfront is lined with sculptures made by artists from all around the world. One bronze sculpture is a ladder with two children climbing it while their mother stands below. Another is

Whimsical sculpture on Circle of the Sea in Puerto Vallarta

JALISCO | MEXICO

a nine-foot-high sea horse with a boy on its back. The Friendship Fountain has three large dolphin sculptures.

"My favorite sculpture was the ladder. Which one did you like best?" Bryce asked.

"I liked the ones by the artist from Guadalajara, Alejandro Colunga. The high-backed chair with the octopus on it was my favorite piece," Avaron responded.

The kids sat by the water and watched the sunset. Banderas Bay is the largest natural bay in Mexico and the second largest in North America. Dolphins swim in its warm waters year-round, and humpback whales visit every winter.

The next morning, Avaron traveled to one of the northern beaches to take a surfing lesson. Bryce stayed where the water was calmer and fished. In the afternoon, the kids wandered through town, looking at the many shops. They were interested in the yarn paintings they saw and asked a shopkeeper about them. She explained that they were made by the Huichol (pronounced *WEE-chol*) Indians. Thought to be descendants of the Aztecs, many of these people live in mountainous areas a few hours from Puerto Vallarta. They are one of the last remaining native cultures in the world that has kept its ancient customs, language, and habitat.

The yarn "paintings," which do not actually involve the use of paint, are made by spreading beeswax or pine sap across a canvas. Brightly colored yarn is then pressed into the wax. Common designs include corn, water, deer, mountains, feathers, and flowers. The art represents the Huichol's ancient traditions and beliefs.

The kids stopped at a food stall and ordered fish tacos for dinner. They went back to the boardwalk and sat among the sculptures, listening to the waves and enjoying the orange and pink glow as the sun set.

Alejandro Colunga

This self-taught artist once studied architecture and worked for a circus. Besides Mexico, his work can be found in Europe, the United States, and South America. One of his works of art is in Portland, Oregon. The bronze sculpture of a man with antlers on his head is ten feet high and three feet wide. The man's lap serves as a seat.

Detailed designs are created by pressing yarn into beeswax on plywood.

Name _____

Date _____

Map Exploration

Use the map to answer each question.

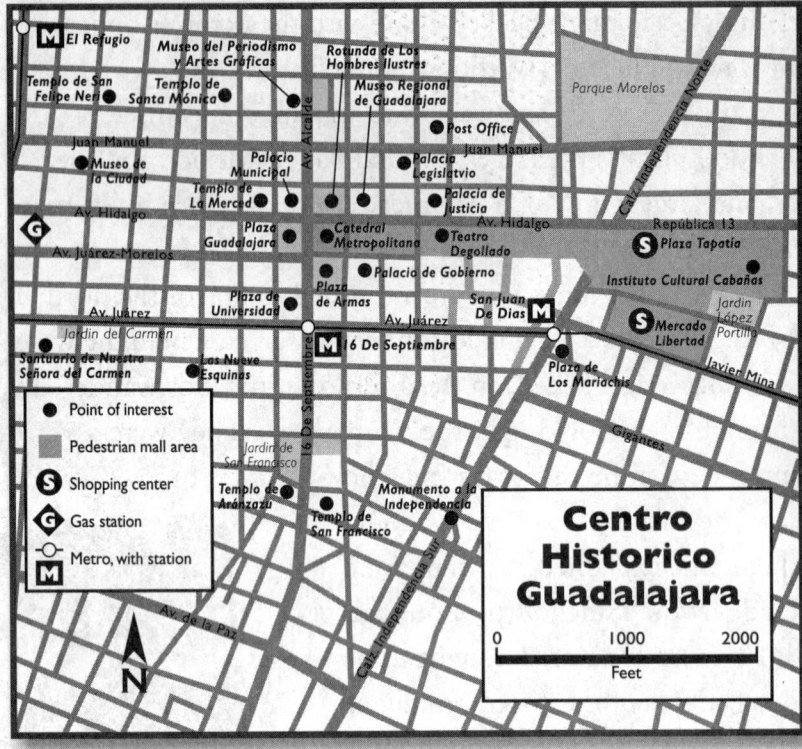

1. Bryce toured the Catedral Metropolitana (Metropolitan Cathedral) while Avaron went shopping at Plaza Topatía. They agreed to meet at a landmark in between that is on the south side of the street. Where will they meet? Who has to walk farther to get there?

   _____
   _____

2. After buying postcards at Plaza Topatía, the kids walked to the post office to mail them. In what direction did they walk?

   _____

3. Where are they? Follow the clues to tell where Bryce and Avaron are.

   A. Bryce and Avaron visited Templo de San Felipe Neri. They walked south about 800 feet and visited a place where they viewed Spanish weapons.

   _____

   B. From there they took a bus east about 2,500 feet just to see the government building on the south side of the street.

   _____

   C. The next day, the kids started at the easternmost Metro station and traveled southwest down Calz Indepencia Sur to find the monument built in 1910 to honor the hundredth anniversary of Mexican independence.

   _____

Vocabulary Voyage

Use the context clues from the passage as a definition. Write the word from the box that goes with its correct context clue.

| cathedral | charro | flan |
| huaraches | mariachi | sombreros |

1. ... wide-brimmed straw hats _____

2. ... a popular sweet custard _____

3. ... a Mexican orchestra _____

4. ... sturdy Mexican sandals _____

5. ... the main church in a district _____

6. ... cowboy _____

Use each word from the box to write a complete sentence.

_____
_____
_____
_____
_____
_____
_____
_____

Name _____

Date _____

Comprehension Expedition

Darken the circle for the best answer.

1. What historical event is celebrated in Mexico every September 16?
   - Ⓐ The 1821 organization of a Mexican government separate from the Spanish
   - Ⓑ The 1810 announcement of Father Hidalgo of a revolution against the Spanish
   - Ⓒ The 1821 adoption of a flag to designate the country of Mexico
   - Ⓓ The 1535 incorporation of Mexico as a colony of Spain

2. The art of Alejandro Colunga can be described as
   - Ⓐ political.
   - Ⓑ serious.
   - Ⓒ amusing.
   - Ⓓ common.

3. What industry is the economy of Puerto Vallarta probably most dependent on?
   - Ⓐ Mining
   - Ⓑ Manufacturing
   - Ⓒ Crafts
   - Ⓓ Tourism

Use complete sentences to answer the question.

4. Is there any evidence of the Aztec people still in Mexico today? If so, where is it located?

_____
_____
_____
_____
_____
_____
_____

LESSON 4: Jalisco Holiday

Name
Date

Writing Adventure

Avaron's friend Mia is active and athletic. Write a letter from Avaron to Mia telling Mia why she'd enjoy a vacation in Puerto Vallarta, Mexico.

Research Navigation

- Use the BBC News country profile Web site on Mexico.

  http://news.bbc.co.uk/1/hi/world/americas/country_profiles/1205074.stm

- Prepare a list of five questions about Mexico.

- Exchange lists with a partner and use the Web site to answer the questions. Questions may be about the country's leaders, economy, facts, history (click on Timeline), or other areas that interest you.

Lesson 5: Reefs, Ruins, and Jaguars

"You know that an asteroid is an object that orbits or moves around the sun, right?" Bryce asked.

"Yes, I know that," Avaron replied.

"Did you know that one hit the Yucatan peninsula about 65 million years ago?" Bryce continued.

"Well, no, I didn't know that," Avaron said.

"And here's the most interesting part: Many scientists believe this asteroid is what caused the extinction of the dinosaurs. The impact from the asteroid blew a hole in our planet that is about 100 miles wide. Much of North America was burned to ashes, due to the angle at which the asteroid struck. The impact created more energy than would be created if all the nuclear weapons on Earth were set off. Earth was covered by a cloud of dust for many years," Bryce explained.

"Wow, that's amazing," Avaron responded. "I've been reading about the history of the area, too, but it doesn't go back quite as far as the dinosaurs. The pre-Columbian Mayan civilization was spread across the Yucatan peninsula. Some of the ruins are 3,000 years old. Unlike the Aztecs, the Maya are alive and well, and millions still live here."

The kids had just flown to the island of Cozumel, located off the eastern coast of the Yucatan Peninsula. The Yucatan Peninsula includes three Mexican

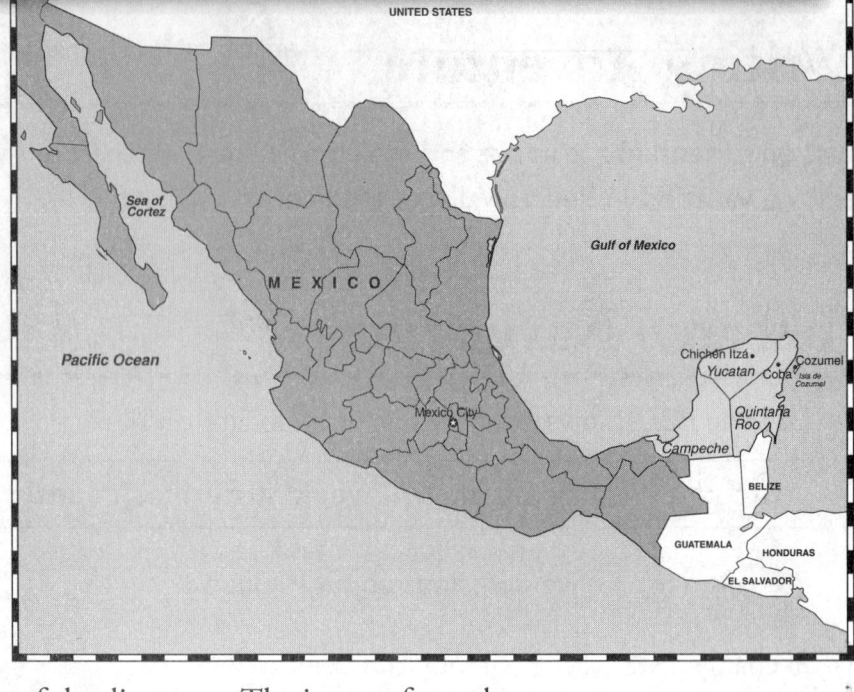

This Mayan ruin overlooks a beautiful beach on the Yucatan peninsula.

YUCATAN PENINSULA | MEXICO

states (Quintana Roo, Yucatan, and Campeche), as well as the nation of Belize and part of Guatemala.

After renting masks, snorkels, and fins, they entered the clear, warm water. Colorful fish darted in and out of the coral. The kids saw an eel and a stingray. Avaron dove down to look at a starfish that was resting on the sand. Bryce followed a large school of fish.

After a while, Bryce tapped Avaron on the shoulder. The kids surfaced and removed their masks and snorkels.

"Guess what?" Bryce asked.

"You're hungry, right?" Avaron responded.

Bryce nodded. Avaron suggested they go to the History Museum, explaining that it had a rooftop restaurant. After eating seafood tacos, they wandered through the exhibits. They learned about the island's plant and animal life. They also found an explanation of coral formation.

Bryce read aloud, "Coral are small sea animals that are related to jellyfish. They don't move during their adulthood. They settle on a rock, another coral, or the ocean's floor. Then they form a type of limestone skeleton. Even after the animal dies, the skeleton remains. Coral reefs are found in relatively shallow water because they must have sunlight. They also need warm water."

"Do you know what leaves marks on the beach that look like a single large tire track?" Avaron asked.

"A large tire?" Bryce guessed.

"No, it's a sea turtle. Two different kinds of turtles come to Cozumel every year to lay their eggs. Turtle meat and eggs have been part of the Mayan diet for hundreds of years. And as you know, tourism has increased dramatically in the Yucatan in recent years. This leads to human invasion of the turtle ecosystem. As a result, there are now some programs that help the turtles to survive. During the nesting season, biologists and volunteers find the nests and move the eggs to safer locations," Avaron explained.

Many loggerhead turtles lay their eggs on Cozumel beaches.

"There sure are lots of cool animals here. This is a good place to study living things," said Bryce.

Avaron nodded in agreement.

YUCATAN PENINSULA | MEXICO

After a few days on Cozumel, the kids went to the mainland. Their first stop was Chichén Itzá (pronounced *chee-CHEN ee-TSA*). This Mayan city was built about 1,500 years ago. It includes a 79-foot-tall pyramid with stairs on all four sides. Architects and astronomers designed the pyramid so that twice a year shadows caused by the setting sun would look like a large snake moving down the steps. One of the Maya's main deities was a serpent with feathers. Artwork showing this god, known as Kukulkan, is found at the top of the pyramid.

The city's 545-foot ball court is the largest in the Americas. Here, the Maya played a game they called pok-ta-pok. The object was to hit a rubber ball through a vertical stone ring. Artwork on the walls of the court shows a man holding the decapitated, or cut-off, head of his opponent. It is unknown if the winner or the loser was sacrificed. Some people believe the winner was sacrificed so that he could go on to play with the gods.

This pyramid is in Chichén Itzá. The hundreds of columns stretch into the jungle.

Along with pyramids and ball courts, another common feature found in many large Mayan cities was cenotes. A cenote (pronounced *si-NO-tee*) is a deep sinkhole in limestone with a pool at the bottom. This natural well was used as a source of water. However, they were also sometimes used for religious purposes. At Chichén Itzá, there are two cenotes. One was used for water, and the other was used as a place to throw offerings to the gods, including precious metals and sometimes people.

The Maya developed a calendar, accurate astronomical observations, and spectacular architecture. In addition to houses, they built large complicated temples. They were the only pre-Columbian civilization in the Americas to develop a complete writing system. Around A.D. 900, their power began to decline, and many of the great cities were abandoned. Still, many cities and towns remained when the Spanish made contact in the 1500s. The Spanish soldiers did not defeat the final independent Mayan city-state until 1697.

The next day, the kids went to the Mayan ruins at Coba. They climbed to the top of the pyramid, which is even higher than the one at Chichén Itzá. Making the journey even more difficult was the fact that many of the steep steps were broken. After reaching the top, they looked out at the surrounding jungle. When it was time to go down, Bryce became very quiet.

"What's wrong?" Avaron asked.

"Those stairs are what's wrong. It's easy enough to climb up this thing,

YUCATAN PENINSULA | MEXICO

because all you see in front of you are more stairs. But going back down, all you see is empty space in front of you and the ground far, far below," Bryce replied.

He solved his problem by sitting down on the top step and scooting slowly to the next step. He proceeded this way until he was about halfway down, when he was comfortable enough to stand up. Avaron tried not to let him see her laughing.

The kids proceeded down the coast until they reached the Sian Ka'an Biosphere Reserve. This area consists of one and a half million acres of protected land, including both forest and sea. Avaron had booked a room at the Visitors' Center, and the kids planned to go on an organized tour, including kayaking, hiking, and snorkeling. Avaron was most excited about seeing a manatee. Bryce was most excited about tracking jaguars.

"The jaguar is the largest cat in the Americas, and the third-largest cat in the world. They're shy animals, and people seldom see them. But maybe we'll get lucky. I *hope* we get lucky," Bryce said.

The tour group went into the jungle. The guide explained what various plants were, pointed out different kinds of monkeys, and found tracks left by a variety of animals on the jungle floor.

After the tour ended, the kids ate dinner. Then they returned to their room. "No jaguars, not even any jaguar tracks," Bryce sighed. He picked up his book, *Jaguars in the Yucatan*.

Before going to bed, Avaron wanted to go outside to look at the stars. She asked Bryce if he wanted to join her.

"No thanks, this book is too good to put down," he replied.

Avaron returned a few minutes later. Her face was pale.

"You're not going to believe this, but I just saw a jaguar," Avaron said quietly.

"What? A jaguar?" Bryce jumped up and ran toward the door.

"Wait, don't go outside! It might not be safe!" Avaron yelled.

"Go outside? Are you crazy?" Bryce asked as he locked the door and checked to make sure the windows were secure. "The word *jaguar* means 'the killer that takes its prey in a single bound.' I'm not going anywhere!"

Manatees

Manatees can grow up to 13 feet long, and they can weigh as much as 1,300 pounds. Still, these water-dwelling mammals, which are related to elephants, are quite graceful. Long ago, some very confused sailors thought these creatures were mermaids!

Several hundred manatees live in Mexican coastal waters.

The Sian Ka'an Biosphere Reserve provides a protected home for the jaguar.

LESSON 5
Reefs, Ruins, and Jaguars

Name _____

Date _____

Map Exploration

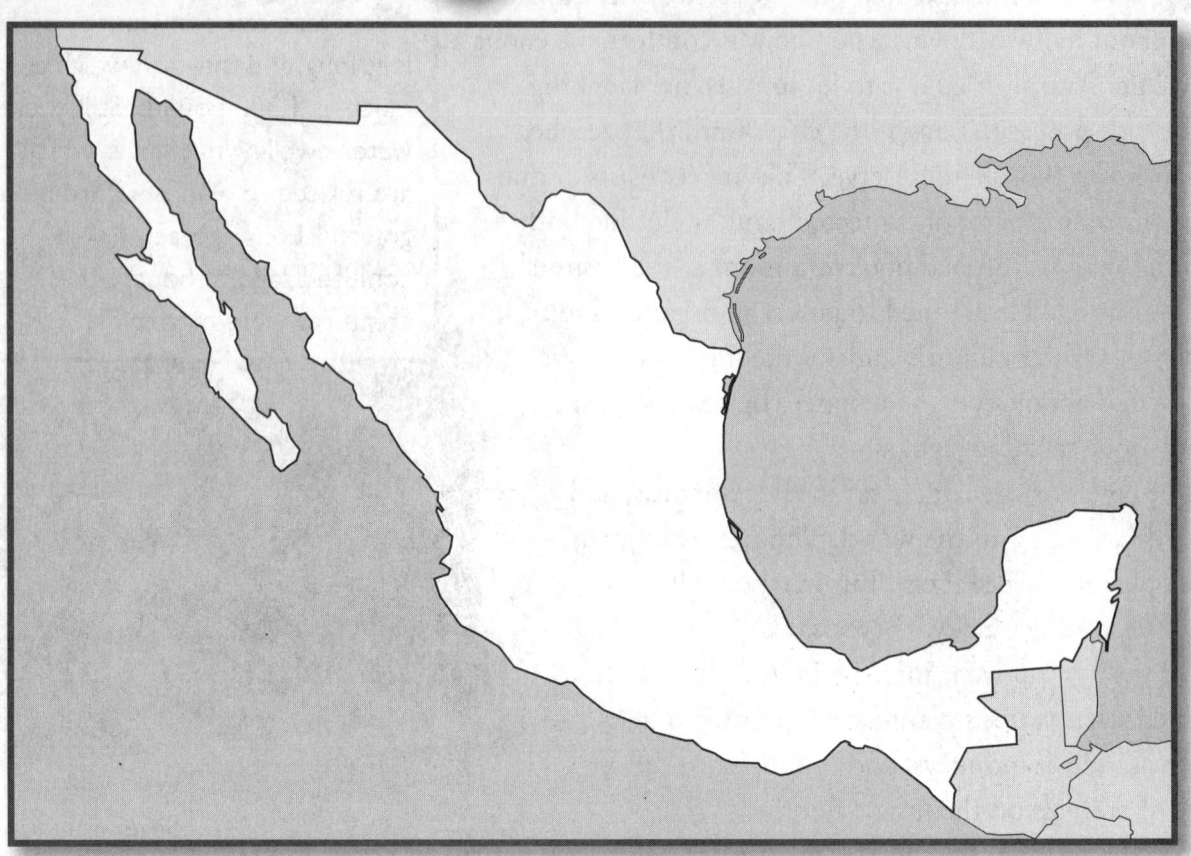

Use an atlas or Internet map site to complete the map of Mexico.

1. Mark the Yucatan peninsula on the map.

2. Mark the Baja peninsula on the map.

3. Put the following cities on the map: Mexico City, Guadalajara, Tijuana, and Chihuahua.

4. Put the Sierra Madre Occidental and the Sierra Madre Del Sur (mountain ranges) on the map.

5. What bodies of water border both Mexico and the United States?

_____

_____

_____

www.harcourtschoolsupply.com
© Harcourt Achieve Inc. All rights reserved.

Mexico: Lesson 5
Journeys Around the World, SV 1419027875

LESSON 5: Reefs, Ruins, and Jaguars

Name _____

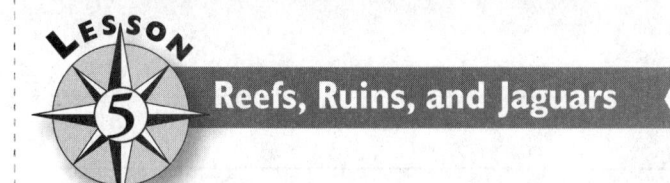

Date _____

Vocabulary Voyage

Write the vocabulary word that fits with the speaker's statement. Use the vocabulary words in the box.

architecture	asteroid	biologist	cenotes
decapitated	deities	extinction	impact

1. "That big rock is circling the sun." _____
2. "I believe all dinosaurs were gone from Earth millions of years ago." _____
3. "When the bomb hit the ground, it made a large crater." _____
4. "That scientist studies the habits of some sea creatures." _____
5. "Quite a bit of pre-Columbian art is decorated with gods and goddesses." _____
6. "It's hard to believe a reward for winning would be getting one's head cut off!" _____
7. "Mayan people carried water from wells deep in limestone back to their homes." _____
8. "Like the Chinese, the Maya decorated some of their buildings with carvings of stone." _____

Use each word in the box to write a complete sentence.

_____
_____
_____
_____
_____

LESSON 5
Reefs, Ruins, and Jaguars

Name _____

Date _____

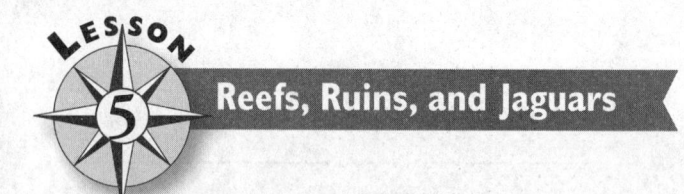

Comprehension Expedition

Darken the circle for the best answer.

1. What historical event happened in the Yucatan long before humans were there?
   - Ⓐ The pre-Columbian Mayan civilization spread across the region.
   - Ⓑ The Mayan city of Chichén Itzá was built, including a large sports court.
   - Ⓒ Jaguars and manatees lived freely all over the peninsula.
   - Ⓓ An asteroid crashed to Earth and caused dinosaurs to become extinct.

2. What is being done in Cozumel to protect turtles?
   - Ⓐ Turtles are being eaten by the Maya.
   - Ⓑ Turtles are being raised on coral reefs.
   - Ⓒ Turtles are being kept in Sian Ka'an Biosphere Reserve.
   - Ⓓ Turtle nests are being moved to safe locations.

3. What evidence indicates the Maya were good astronomers?
   - Ⓐ They built a structure that created artistic shadows when the sun hit it a certain way.
   - Ⓑ They were able to develop a ball game called pok-ta-pok.
   - Ⓒ They were able to develop a complete writing system.
   - Ⓓ They were not defeated by the Spanish until the late 1600s.

Use complete sentences to answer the question.

4. What are two things the Mayan people were good at? Support your answer with examples from the passage.

_____
_____
_____
_____
_____
_____
_____

www.harcourtschoolsupply.com
© Harcourt Achieve Inc. All rights reserved.

44

Mexico: Lesson 5
Journeys Around the World, SV 1419027875

LESSON 5
REEFS, RUINS, AND JAGUARS

Name _____

Date _____

Writing Adventure

Which rare animal would you be most excited to see: sea turtle, manatee, or jaguar? Why do you feel this way? Write a paragraph to support your answer.

Research Navigation

This lesson completes Bryce and Avaron's trip to Mexico. Two important pre-Columbian civilizations in Mexico were the Aztec and the Maya. Complete the following chart to compare the two empires. Use the Internet to find the information.

	Maya	Aztec
Geographic Location		
Religious Beliefs and Practices		
Role of Slavery		
Weapons Used in Warfare		

LESSON 6: Walking in Viking Footsteps

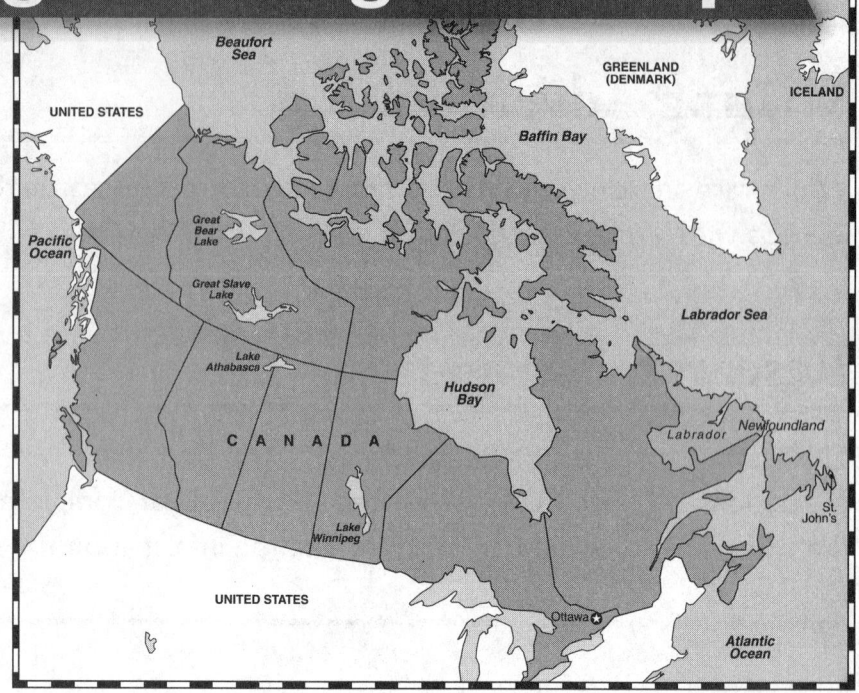

"OK, now that we've arrived in the Canadian province of Newfoundland and Labrador, I know you're just dying to make a joke about the fact that both places share their names with dog breeds," Avaron said.

"No jokes, but I have done some research about the dogs. The Labrador retriever actually originated in Newfoundland. The Newfoundland did, too, though it would be funny if that breed originated in Labrador. Anyway, the two breeds are related. They both have webbed feet and water-repellent coats. They were used to help the fishermen, since this area has always supported itself by fishing. Both breeds are strong swimmers, and they were used to retrieve everything—fish that fell off hooks, fishing nets, small boats, even people," Bryce commented.

"Yeah, I read that the Grand Banks, located off the southeast coast of Newfoundland, is one of the richest fishing grounds in the world," Avaron noted.

"That's also the area where the *Titanic* sank in 1912," Bryce said.

Canada is made up of ten provinces and three territories. The province of Newfoundland and Labrador consists of a section of the mainland (Labrador) and a large island (Newfoundland). More than 90 percent of the population of this province lives on the island, which is known as "The Rock."

Few people live in Labrador due to its severe climate. However, a significant number of Inuit

The capital city of St. John's

people live here. The Inuit used to be called Eskimos. These hardy people have survived in the Arctic region for more than 2,000 years.

"Did you know that Canada is the second-largest country in the world?" Avaron asked.

"Yeah, and its government is a confederation with a parliamentary democracy. Similar to the United States, some of Canada's provinces were originally British colonies. Today, the chief of state is the queen of England, but the head of the government is the Canadian prime minister. This is different from the U.S., where the president is both chief of state and head of the government," Bryce noted.

The kids were in St. John's, the capital and largest city of the province. One of the foggiest and windiest cities in Canada, St. John's is located on the eastern side of the island.

"It's chilly out here. Let's go in that restaurant to get warm," Bryce said.

"You wouldn't want to eat while we're in there, would you?" Avaron asked, knowing that Bryce was almost always hungry.

Bryce ordered one of Newfoundland's special dishes: cod tongue. Avaron had a fish sandwich. She looked at a map of the province.

"I love the names people gave to the places around here. How would you like to live in Jerry's Nose? Or maybe Blow Me Down, or Gripe Point," she said.

"Let me see that," Bryce replied.

She handed him the map. As he read, he began to laugh.

"I'd rather live in Happy Adventure. Look, another place is called Goobies! And there's Come by Chance, Main Tickle, and Ha Ha Bay," he said.

After finishing lunch, the kids went to Pippy Park. Here they visited a unique site called the Fluvarium. The name means "windows on a stream." It is an educational program to teach people about preserving freshwater habitats. There are nine underwater windows where visitors can watch the native stream life, including trout and frogs, as they swim by.

Their next activity was a boat tour of Witless Bay Ecological Reserve. Made up of four islands, the reserve is the nesting ground for over two million sea birds. Among them is the official bird of the province, the puffin. This black and white bird has bright orange feet and a multicolored beak.

"Oh, I love the puffins. They're so cute!" Avaron said.

The Titanic

The *Titanic* was a British ocean liner. The ship was making its first journey, sailing from England to the United States, when it hit an iceberg and sank. This took place a few hundred miles off the coast of Newfoundland. Over 1,500 people were lost at sea in the tragedy.

Atlantic puffins are found only in North America in the North Atlantic Ocean. Their nesting grounds range from Labrador to the northeastern United States. Most of the world's puffins are found in Iceland.

NEWFOUNDLAND / LABRADOR | CANADA

"I like watching them try to fly. They're fine once they get going, but they sure are awkward with the takeoff," Bryce commented. The kids watched as a puffin skipped and stumbled along the shore, looking a bit like a windup toy.

While on the tour, the kids also saw humpback whales. One whale slapped its tail on the water's surface, making a loud cracking sound. Others stuck their heads up from the water for a few seconds.

An endangered species, the 50-foot whale lives up to 50 years. It breeds in warm southern waters during the winter and then travels north during the summer to feed. It makes a wide range of sounds, or songs, some lasting up to half an hour.

"Look at the icebergs," said Bryce.

"That one looks like a floating castle," Avaron commented, pointing to one of the larger icebergs.

Icebergs are pieces of glaciers that break off and float in the sea. The visible part is only a small fraction of the overall size. While icebergs are beautiful, they can be very dangerous to ships traveling nearby.

After returning to St. John's, the kids went to Cape Spear National Historic Site. They saw the oldest surviving lighthouse in Newfoundland, located at the most eastern point of the continent.

The next day, they traveled to L'Anse aux Meadows. This is the site of a thousand-year-old Viking settlement. The Vikings were from the Scandinavian region of Europe. They traveled by sea and often raided European coastal communities during the eighth, ninth, and tenth centuries. L'Anse aux Meadows was the first European settlement in North America. Located on the northern tip of the island, the site looks out on the bay. The settlement consisted of eight sod buildings. Copies of the buildings have been made so that visitors can experience the site as it was when the Vikings lived here.

Glaciers form on land and slowly move or flow. When the edge of the glacier gets to the ocean, a piece breaks off. That piece is an iceberg.

NEWFOUNDLAND / LABRADOR | CANADA

"It's amazing to see where the Vikings lived so long ago," Bryce noted. He took a photo of one of the guides, who was dressed in clothing like the Vikings used to wear.

"Yes, it is. But the Vikings weren't the first people to live here. They were just the first Europeans to live here. A group of hunter-gatherers called the Beothuk were the original inhabitants. Unfortunately, they all died out by the mid-nineteenth century," Avaron noted.

"And the Vikings only stayed here for two or three years. The next Europeans didn't arrive for another five hundred years. In 1497, John Cabot showed up. He was an Italian who had moved to England. About one hundred years later, England claimed Newfoundland as its first overseas colony," Bryce said.

The kids traveled on to Gros Morne National Park. Located on the western side of the island, the park is home to caribou, moose, black bears, and humpback whales. Visitors can hike through the mountains or along the sea.

There are also many bogs in the park. Pitcher plants, which are the official flower of the province, grow in this soft, wet land. These plants don't get enough nutrients from the bog, so they have developed a way to capture bugs and other small creatures. The plants have little pitchers containing a sweet liquid that attracts insects. The insects crawl in, but they can't climb back out. The plant digests the bugs.

"Wow, seeing those pitcher plants makes me hungry," said Bryce. "Let's go find some cod tongue for dinner!"

Sod Buildings

Sod is dirt bound by grasses and roots. After building a timber frame, the Vikings (as well as many other settlers) put strips of sod in place, completing the structure. Sod buildings are known to stay cool in the summer and warm in the winter.

In addition to its use as a building material for the first European settlement in North America, sod was also used by settlers in the prairie west.

Lesson 6: Walking in Viking Footsteps

Name _____

Date _____

Chart the Course

Use the table to answer each question.

2001 Population in Canada (to the nearest thousand)	
Alberta	2,975,000
British Columbia	3,908,000
Manitoba	1,120,000
New Brunswick	729,000
Newfoundland and Labrador	513,000
Northwest Territories	37,000
Nova Scotia	908,000
Nunavut	27,000
Ontario	11,410,000
Prince Edward Island	135,000
Québec	7,237,000
Saskatchewan	979,000
Yukon Territory	29,000
CANADA TOTAL	30,007,000

1. If you were to make a bar graph of this information, which province or territory would have the longest bar?

   _____

2. On your bar graph, which two provinces or territories would have the shortest bars? Using a map, speculate why so few people live in these two regions.

   _____
   _____
   _____
   _____

3. Bryce suggests they "get away from it all." Which province or territory might he pick to get away from the most people?

   _____

4. Newfoundland and Labrador and Nova Scotia border the Atlantic Ocean. British Columbia borders the Pacific Ocean. Which part of Canada is more populated, the Atlantic coast or the Pacific coast?

   _____

LESSON 6: Walking in Viking Footsteps

Name _____

Date _____

Vocabulary Voyage

Use each vocabulary term in the box to complete the sentence.

| bog | parliamentary democracy | glacier | Inuit |
| iceberg | provinces and territories | sod | |

1. The huge mass of ice and snow began to melt. As the _____ melted, it moved slowly across land.

2. The _____ broke off the huge mass of ice and snow and floated in the ocean.

3. The United States is made up of 50 states. Canada is made up of thirteen _____ .

4. The settler dug up a section of grass and roots to use to build the _____ house.

5. As soon as he stepped on the wet, spongy ground, he knew he'd found the _____ .

6. The _____ are the native people of the Arctic region of Canada.

7. Since Ottawa is the capital of Canada, it houses the government offices of the _____ .

Use each vocabulary term in the box to write a complete sentence of your own.

_____
_____
_____

Lesson 6: Walking in Viking Footsteps

Name _____

Date _____

Comprehension Expedition

Darken the circle for the best answer.

1. What industry supports the economy of Newfoundland and Labrador?
   - Ⓐ Tourism
   - Ⓑ Housing
   - Ⓒ Fishing
   - Ⓓ Manufacturing

2. How can an iceberg be dangerous?
   - Ⓐ It can be an obstacle to ships.
   - Ⓑ It can melt and cause floods.
   - Ⓒ It can move down a mountain.
   - Ⓓ It can cause cold, deadly weather.

3. What Europeans were the first to build a settlement in North America?
   - Ⓐ English
   - Ⓑ Vikings
   - Ⓒ French
   - Ⓓ Italians

Use complete sentences to answer the questions.

4. Canada is divided into _____, while the United States is divided into _____ .

5. How are the leaders of Canada and the United States different?
   _____
   _____
   _____
   _____

6. How are Canadian and U.S. history similar?
   _____
   _____

LESSON 6: Walking in Viking Footsteps

Name _____

Date _____

Writing Adventure

In a paragraph, compare and contrast the weather in Newfoundland and Labrador with the weather in your community. You can use information in this passage and information from other sources. How are the climates similar and how are they different? Which climate do you prefer? State reasons for your opinion.

Research Navigation

- Go to the Geography section of the oCanada Web site to make a Canadian Quiz.

  http://www.ocanada.ca/

- Read through the information about Canada's geography. Use the information on the Web site to prepare three questions.

- Exchange questions with a partner and use the Web site to answer the questions.

LESSON 7: Mostly Québec

"Hey, there it is," said Bryce, pointing at a large stone house. He and Avaron were in Montréal, Canada's second-largest city. They were staying at a bed-and-breakfast located in the heart of town.

"I'm excited to stay in a bed-and-breakfast. It will be nice to rent a room in someone's home instead of staying in a motel," Avaron said.

"It will be nice to have someone cook breakfast for us in the morning, too!" said Bryce.

The kids walked inside and were greeted by a loud voice that said, "Bienvenue à Montréal!" ("Welcome to Montréal!")

"Merci," Avaron replied, saying "Thank you" in French.

"Ah, you are Americans. I will speak English for you," said François, their host. He and his wife, Jacqueline, owned the bed-and-breakfast.

Montréal is located in the province of Québec, Canada's largest province. The official language is French. Montréal is one of the world's largest French-speaking cities, second only to Paris, France.

After putting their backpacks in their room, the kids found François and asked him if he had any sightseeing recommendations.

"Oh, yes, there is much for you to see and do here. Perhaps you would like to start at Mount Royal, the mountain park created in 1876. It was designed by the same man who designed New York's Central Park. The mountain is how our city got its name, because it used to be called Mont Réal," François noted.

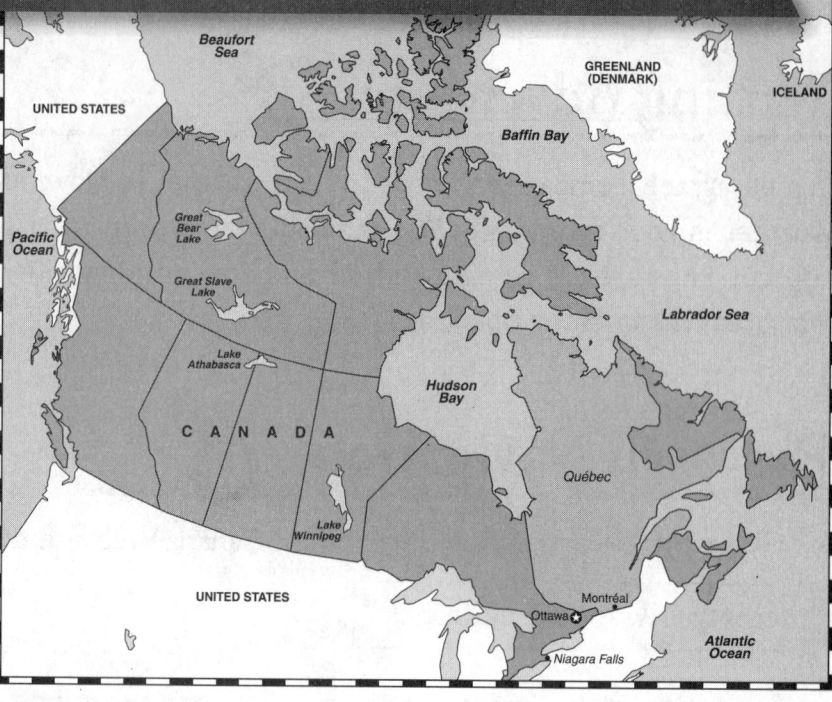

The modern city of Montréal as seen from Mount Royal

QUÉBEC | CANADA

Bryce and Avaron agreed to visit the park. They enjoyed the views of the city, which is on an island. It is located where the Saint Lawrence and Ottawa rivers meet.

"The Huron Indians, along with other tribes, had lived here for thousands of years before the first Europeans arrived in 1535. The new explorers claimed the land for the French king," Avaron noted.

"Another Frenchman, Samuel de Champlain, explored the area in 1603. The French established the first permanent settlement here in 1642," Bryce added.

"And it remained under French control until 1760, when the French surrendered it to the British at the end of the French and Indian War," Avaron said.

"The mixture of French and British cultures makes the province of Québec unique. It has also led to some serious disagreements and attempts to establish Québec as a French-speaking nation, separate from Canada," said Bryce.

"Yes, I read that in 1995, the people voted to remain part of Canada, but the vote was very close. More than 98 percent of the people who could vote did so. Just a little more than 49 percent wanted independence, while just a little more than 50 percent wanted to remain part of Canada. That's about as close as you can get!" Avaron said.

After admiring the views and strolling through the park, the kids proceeded to Olympic Park. Originally built for the 1976 Olympics, the park is now used for a number of other things. Visitors can attend concerts, participate in sports activities, or eat at one of the restaurants here. The kids went up the Montréal Tower, which is the tallest inclined tower in the world. It was purposely built at a slant. It leans at a 45-degree angle.

"Wow! I thought we had a good view from Mount Royal, but this is really amazing!" Bryce exclaimed.

"Yeah, the guidebook says you can see for 50 miles on a clear day," Avaron noted.

This tower was built to lean at a 45-degree angle. It leans over the Olympic stadium.

QUÉBEC | CANADA

Their next stop was a nearby attraction called the Insectarium. The outside of the building is designed to look like an insect. The nearby gardens are designed to attract insects. And inside are exhibits of both live and mounted bugs. The center is designed to provide information and to conduct research. After touring the building, the kids were gathering their things and getting ready to leave.

"I'm just sorry we're not here in November or December," Bryce commented.

"Really? Why?" Avaron asked.

"Because that's when they have the annual Insect Tasting. They make all kinds of fancy snacks out of bugs, things like jellied crickets and barbecued locusts!" Bryce replied.

Avaron rolled her eyes. Before she could ask him if there was anything he wouldn't eat, he had disappeared into the gift shop. He came out carrying a bag and grinning. He pulled a mealworm sucker out of the bag and unwrapped it. Before popping it in his mouth, he told Avaron they sold chocolate-covered crickets.

"Insects are a good source of protein, and they contain minerals and vitamins. Don't you want to try some?" he asked.

"No. Unlike you, I don't feel obligated to eat everything I see," she replied.

When Bryce didn't reply, Avaron turned around to look at him. He had a disgusted expression on his face. He took the sucker out of his mouth and dropped it in a nearby trash can.

"OK, I no longer feel obligated to eat mealworms," Bryce said, as Avaron laughed.

Next, the kids went to the Biodome. This unique museum, whose name means "life house," contains four ecosystems of the Americas. An ecosystem is a group of plants and animals and its environment. The Biodome contains a tropical forest, a Laurentian forest, a marine ecosystem, and a polar ecosystem. It is home to more than 6,000 animals and more than 4,000 plants.

Although tropical rain forests cover only a small part of Earth's surface, they are home to half to two-thirds of the planet's known plant and animal species. Laurentian forests are northern forests that contain both evergreens and trees whose leaves change seasonally. The marine ecosystems have fish and birds that live in or near cold saltwater. The polar ecosystem includes both an Arctic and an Antarctic section.

King penguins live in the Antarctic ecosystem at the Montréal Biodome.

QUÉBEC | CANADA

At the end of their tour, Bryce asked Avaron what she had liked the best. "Being able to watch the beavers inside their den, thanks to the video camera that has been placed inside, was amazing," she replied. Bryce agreed, although he said the piranhas and bats that he saw in the rain forest were his favorite things.

The kids returned to the bed-and-breakfast to get ready for their journey to Niagara Falls the following morning. Since it is located eight hours away from the city, in the neighboring province of Ontario, they would ride the bus one day, visit the falls the next, and return the third day for more time in Montréal.

Niagara is an Iroquois Indian word meaning "thunder of waters." Located between Ontario and New York, these falls drain four of the Great Lakes. The water above the falls is directed into channels and used to produce power in hydroelectric plants.

"The falls are about 160 feet high. They are split into two sections by an island. On the Canadian side, they are 2,600 feet wide. On the American side, they are 1,000 feet wide. Almost 380,000 tons of water pours off the cliffs every minute. And still, there are people who are crazy enough to go over the falls!" said Bryce.

"Yeah, most of the people who have tried to survive the drop have gone over in barrels. Some of them survived, but many others did not," noted Avaron.

"One guy went over the falls on a jet ski. He was wearing a parachute, but it didn't work properly. Needless to say, he was killed," Bryce commented.

"A couple of people have made the drop wearing only the clothes on their back. One did it by accident, after the motorboat he was in developed mechanical problems. But another guy did it on purpose. And he lived to tell about it. He was fined $2,300," said Avaron.

"People do some strange things," Bryce noted. "And while I don't have any desire to plunge down Niagara Falls, I sure am looking forward to seeing it."

Hydroelectricity

Hydroelectric power is electricity that is produced by fast-moving water. Many hydroelectric plants are located by big dams on big rivers. Hydroelectricity is a clean source of energy. However, the construction of large dams can damage marine life. About 70 percent of Canada's electricity is generated from water sources.

Millions of tourists visit Niagara Falls each year.

LESSON 7: Mostly Québec

Name _____
Date _____

Map Exploration

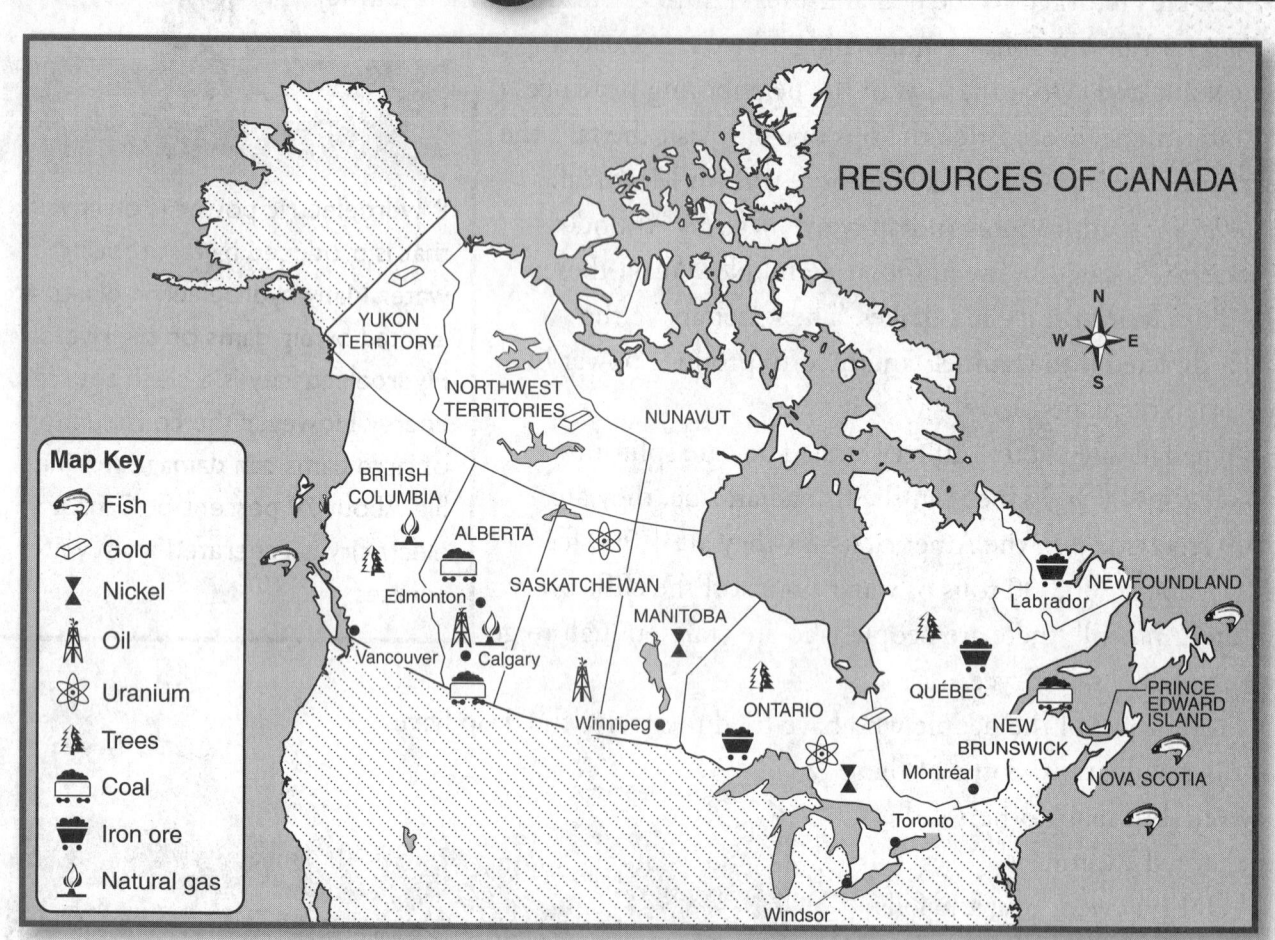

RESOURCES OF CANADA

Map Key
- Fish
- Gold
- Nickel
- Oil
- Uranium
- Trees
- Coal
- Iron ore
- Natural gas

Use the resource map to answer the questions.

1. The United States imports oil from Canada. From which two provinces is the oil most likely exported? _____

2. Avaron would like to visit a gold mine while in Canada. Where should she go to see one? _____

3. What are three natural resources of British Columbia? _____

4. What industry employs people in New Brunswick? _____

LESSON 7: Mostly Québec

Name _____
Date _____

Vocabulary Voyage

Use the words in the box and the clues to complete the puzzle.

| angle | channel | ecosystem | generate |
| hydroelectric | incline | obligate | sightseeing |

Across
1. a narrow sea of water between two areas of land deep and wide enough for ships to use
5. visiting interesting places
7. a kind of power produced by flowing water
8. to force someone to do something by law or because it is right

Down
2. all the living things and their environment in a natural setting
3. to lean or slope
4. the space formed by two lines extending from the same point
6. to produce

www.harcourtschoolsupply.com
© Harcourt Achieve Inc. All rights reserved.

59

Canada: Lesson 7
Journeys Around the World, SV 1419027875

LESSON 7 — Mostly Québec

Name _____

Date _____

Comprehension Expedition

Darken the circle for the best answer.

1. How did the city of Montréal get its name?
   - Ⓐ From an Indian tribe
   - Ⓑ From a mountain
   - Ⓒ From a French explorer
   - Ⓓ From New York's Central Park

2. What conflict was closely resolved in 1995?
   - Ⓐ France gave control of Québec to England.
   - Ⓑ Québec remained a province of Canada.
   - Ⓒ Québec became an independent nation.
   - Ⓓ French became the official language of Canada.

3. Where does Canada get most of its energy?
   - Ⓐ Oil
   - Ⓑ Sun
   - Ⓒ Timber
   - Ⓓ Water

Use complete sentences to answer the question.

4. How does Niagara Falls contribute to the Canadian economy?

_____
_____
_____
_____
_____
_____
_____

Lesson 8: Manitoba in the Middle

"Here we are, in the middle of Canada," Bryce noted, after he and Avaron arrived in the province of Manitoba.

"Manitoba used to be called the Postage Stamp Province, because it was just a small square of land when it became part of Canada. It's grown a lot since then, from 10,000 square miles to 250,000 square miles," Avaron noted.

The kids were in Winnipeg, Manitoba's capital. They entered the Manitoba Museum and found themselves staring into the eyes of a group of galloping bison. The bison were part of a diorama, an exhibit with realistic natural surroundings and a painted background.

Other dioramas included polar bears, moose, native people, and early settlers. The museum also had a full-size copy of a British ship called *Nonsuch*. This ship sailed into Hudson Bay in 1668. The men on board came in search of furs, and they found a huge supply of fur-bearing animals in this part of Canada.

Hudson Bay is an inland sea that borders several Canadian provinces, including Manitoba. It is connected with the Atlantic Ocean, and many large rivers flow into it. Two years after the *Nonsuch* arrived, the British established the Hudson's Bay Company. These fur-trading stations operated for more than 300 years. The company also owned

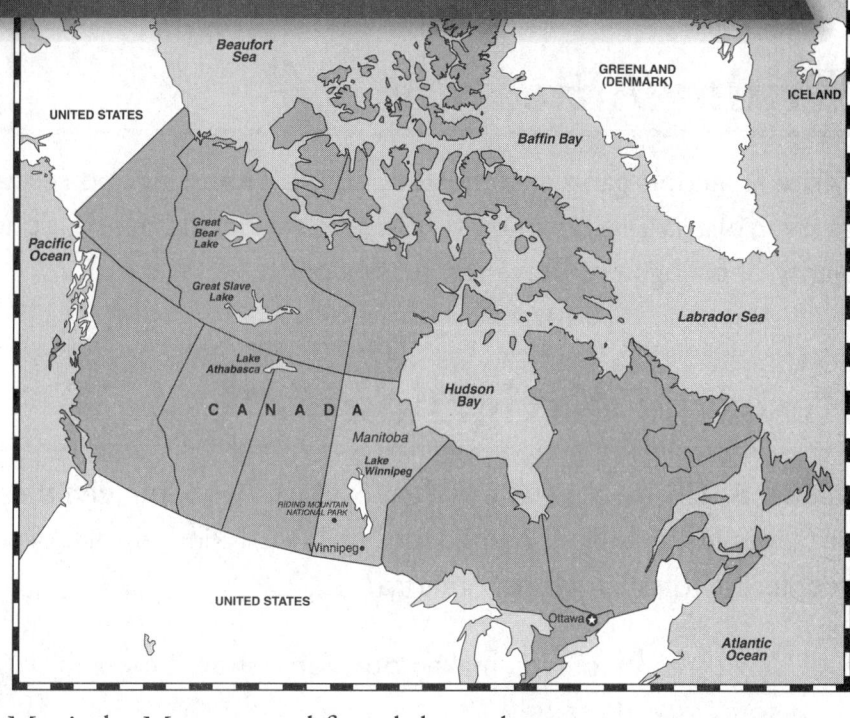

Herds of bison once roamed the Great Plains region of North America, including Manitoba.

LESSON 7: Mostly Québec

Name _____

Date _____

Writing Adventure

Write an action-packed short story about witnessing and rescuing someone who has decided to go over Niagara Falls in a barrel. Be sure to include descriptions of the falls, action sequences, and plenty of dialogue to move the story along.

Research Navigation

Samuel de Champlain was a French explorer who founded the city of Montréal. What place or places in Canada are named for him? What kind of relationship did he have with the native peoples he found in North America?

- Using three resources, make notes for a short biography of Samuel de Champlain. List the resources you used.

- Keep in mind the following:

  1. What is good biographical source material? Who can you ask for help? Where will you look?

  2. How will you organize your notes? Do they lend themselves to an outline? A graphic organizer such as a time line? Short paragraphs?

  3. What parts of Champlain's life are most important to include in a biography?

  4. What is the best way to present the material?

a tremendous amount of land, including parts of five present-day provinces.

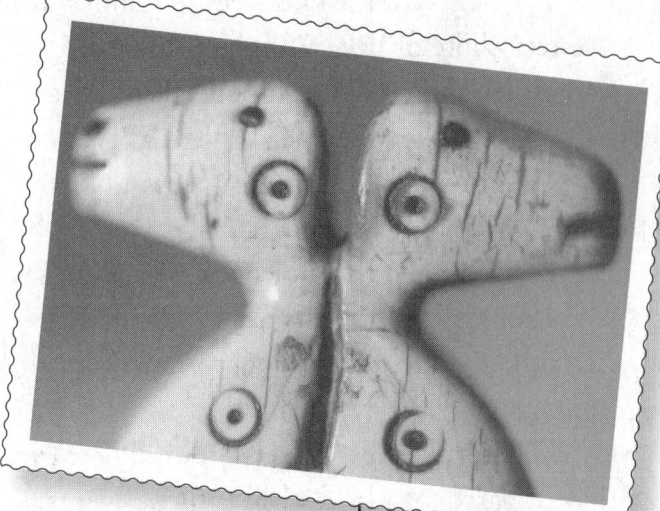

The kids' next stop was the Winnipeg Art Gallery. It includes both historic and modern Canadian art, as well as works by European artists. However, their main interest was the large collection of Inuit art.

"It's fascinating to learn about people's lives through their art," Avaron commented.

Bryce agreed, as they stood and studied a drawing that showed a group of people at sea hunting walruses and seals.

"Let's go to the restaurant across the street and have some dinner," Bryce suggested as they left the museum.

"As long as it's not one of your crazy suggestions, where they serve something like boiled caribou hooves," Avaron replied.

"How about some fresh fish from Manitoba's many lakes?" Bryce asked.

"That sounds good to me," said Avaron.

After eating, the kids went to their room to plan the next day's activities. In the morning, they traveled to Whiteshell Provincial Park, two hours east of the city. They hiked by the park's waterfalls, and they saw several beaver dams along the river. They also visited a place where hundreds of geese stop each year during their migrations. About 150 stay all summer, and about a dozen pairs nest there.

Inuit artists made sculptures of animals found in their region.

"In 1939, a local mink rancher agreed to raise four baby Canadian geese that had been found. He took good care of them, and after they grew up, they migrated south. But they returned each year, and now many other geese stop here, too," Avaron said.

The kids saw petroforms during their afternoon hike. Petroforms are rocks arranged in shapes of snakes, turtles, and people. Others are arranged in geometric designs. Created by Manitoba's original residents, the rock designs were believed to be a way to communicate with the spirits.

The Whiteshell River in Whiteshell Provincial Park

MANITOBA | CANADA

The next day, the kids went to Gimli. Located on the western shore of Lake Winnipeg, the town is home to the largest Icelandic population outside of Iceland.

"Wow, Lake Winnipeg is huge," Bryce commented.

"Yes, it's one of the largest lakes in North America. It's 264 miles long," Avaron said.

Bryce opened his guidebook. "So, Gimli was settled in the 1800s by immigrants from Iceland. They called it New Iceland, and it had its own government for many years," he said.

"There is a huge Icelandic festival here every August. They have a parade, a film festival, athletic events, and contests. Too bad we are here too early to see it," Avaron commented.

The kids went to the beach. Avaron signed up for a windsurfing lesson. Bryce put on his headphones and spread his towel on the white sand. He napped while the waves lapped on the shore. After their day in the sun, Avaron suggested they try some perogies for dinner.

"What's that?" Bryce asked.

"Perogies are dough filled with all kinds of different ingredients, like potatoes and onions and bacon," Avaron replied. "I believe they're from Eastern Europe, but they're popular in Iceland, so they should be easy to find here."

"That sounds great. I'm always ready to try something new," Bryce replied.

The next day, the kids left for Riding Mountain National Park. As they approached the park, Bryce said, "I can see why this place is described as an island of forest in a sea of farmland."

They rented mountain bikes and rode into the forest to the site of a German prisoner-of-war camp. Built during World War II, the camp was so far away from everything that no fences or walls were used. The prisoners cut firewood that was needed by Canadian citizens. The labor normally would have been provided by Canadian workers, but this was not possible because so many Canadians were fighting in Europe. The prisoners received 50 cents a day for their labor.

A Viking sculpture in Gimli

This camp was used to house German prisoners from 1943 to 1945 during World War II.

"It's kind of hard to imagine prisoner-of-war camps in North America," said Bryce.

"It's kind of hard to imagine how much wildlife is in this park, too," Avaron noted. "We should get back to our cabin before it gets dark."

The following day, June 21, was National Aboriginal Day. It is a day to celebrate the unique cultures and contributions of the earliest inhabitants of Canada. These aboriginal or native groups include First Nations, Inuit, and Métis people.

"I know that the Inuit are the people that have lived in the Arctic regions for 2,000 years. And I'm guessing that First Nations refers to the native groups, similar to Native Americans. But who are the Métis?" Bryce asked.

"*Métis* is the French word for 'mixed.' When European and native people married, they mixed the two cultures and their children were called Métis," Avaron explained.

The celebration in the park included displays of art and tools, demonstrations of fishing and trapping, and a food tasting. Bryce was most excited about this final event, though he was disappointed to find that there were no strange foods involved. Still, he enjoyed tasting the foods common to the native groups, such as wild rice, corn, fish, and caribou meat.

Following the celebration, the kids went hiking. Bryce was thumbing through his wildlife tracking book as he walked.

"Riding Mountain National Park is home to wolves, bison, elk, moose, cougars, and a number of smaller animals," he said.

"Sh. Stop," said Avaron.

"Huh? Why? What are you doing?" Bryce asked, looking at Avaron as she quietly pulled her camera out of her backpack.

"It also has a large population of black bears," she said, snapping a photo of a bear ambling across the path in front of them.

"Whoa! Cool!" Bryce exclaimed. "We should come back to Manitoba during October when the polar bears gather around the town of Churchill."

"You'd be so busy reading about them, you'd probably bump right into a bear's mouth," Avaron laughed.

A Famous Bear

The famous bear Winnie the Pooh was a fictional character created by A. A. Milne. However, the character was inspired by a real-life bear. Before World War I, a Canadian soldier was preparing to go overseas. He saw a man at a train station with a black bear cub. The man, a hunter, had killed the cub's mother. The soldier bought the cub. He named the bear "Winnipeg" (after his hometown) and took it to England. He donated the bear to the London Zoo. It was here that Milne's son, Christopher Robin, fell in love with the bear. As a result, he named his stuffed teddy bear Winnie.

LESSON 8: Manitoba in the Middle

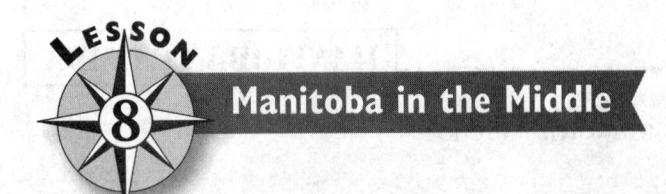

Name _____

Date _____

Map Exploration

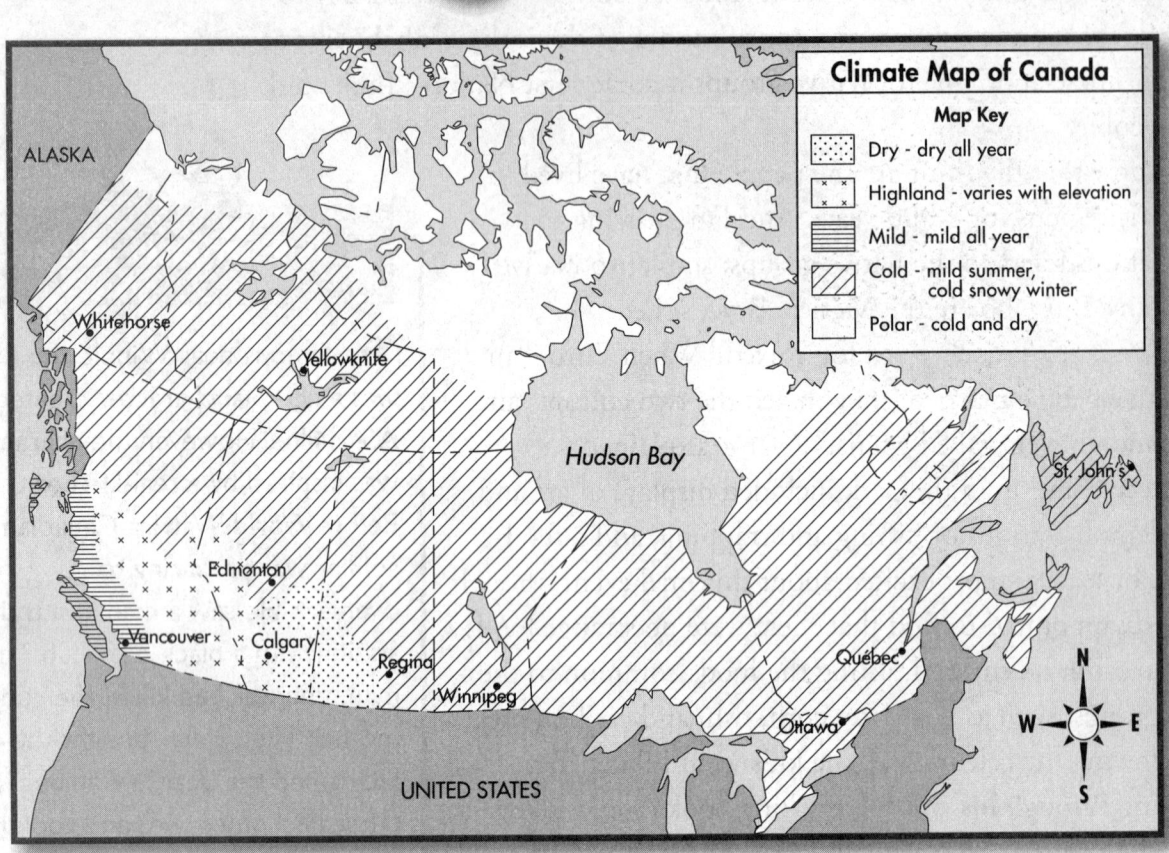

Climate Map of Canada

Map Key
- Dry - dry all year
- Highland - varies with elevation
- Mild - mild all year
- Cold - mild summer, cold snowy winter
- Polar - cold and dry

Use the map to answer each question.

1. What are the five climates shown on this map? _____

2. What kind of climate does most of Canada have? _____

3. What kind of climate does Vancouver have? _____

4. How is the climate in the northern part of Canada different from the climate in the southern part?

5. List the cities on the map that have a mild summer and a cold snowy winter.

LESSON 8: Manitoba in the Middle

Name _____

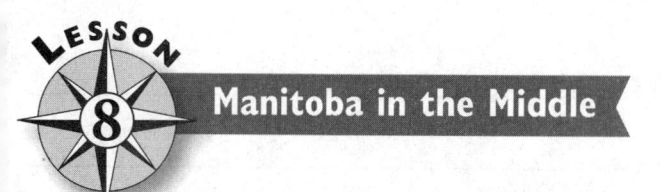

Date _____

Vocabulary Voyage

Read the clue. Write the vocabulary term from the box that completes the book title.

| aboriginal | bison | dioramas | Hudson's Bay Company |
| immigrants | Métis | perogies | petroforms |

1. history of British fur trading in Canada — A History of the _____

2. collection of art by native peoples of Canada — _____ Art

3. how-to book on making three-dimensional exhibits — Building _____

4. a family relocates from China to Canada — A Journey of _____

5. how to make filled pastry treats — Recipes for _____

6. photographs of rocks arranged in spiritual designs — Pictures of _____

7. location of large buffalo-like animals — _____ of North America

8. a girl traces her family history back to both French and Native-American roots — My _____ Family

Use each vocabulary term from the box to write a complete sentence of your own.

_____
_____
_____
_____

LESSON 8
Manitoba in the Middle

Name _____

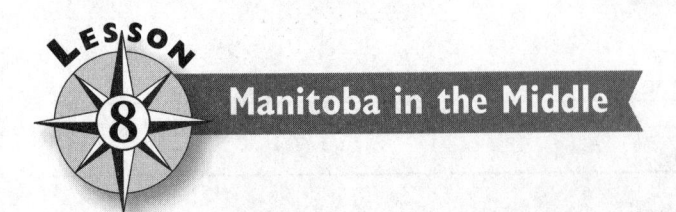

Date _____

Comprehension Expedition

Darken the circle for the best answer.

1. What animal occupied the plains in central Canada?
   - Ⓐ Fish
   - Ⓑ Reptiles
   - Ⓒ Bison
   - Ⓓ Icelandic animals

2. What brought British fur traders to what is now Manitoba?
   - Ⓐ Timber around Hudson Bay
   - Ⓑ Unique Inuit art
   - Ⓒ Amazing petroforms
   - Ⓓ An abundance of fur-bearing animals

3. How could prisoners be kept without walls in what is now Riding Mountain National Park?
   - Ⓐ They were in an isolated forest with nowhere to run to.
   - Ⓑ They were being kept on an island they couldn't escape from.
   - Ⓒ They stayed for the money they made.
   - Ⓓ They were glad to take the jobs of Canadians.

Use complete sentences to answer the question.

4. How do you know Canada is a country that celebrates its multicultural heritage?

_____
_____
_____
_____
_____
_____
_____

LESSON 8: Manitoba in the Middle

Name _____

Date _____

Writing Adventure

Imagine that Bryce promised his cousin that he'd write once a week. On a separate sheet of paper, write a short letter from Bryce to his cousin describing his favorite part of the trip to Canada so far. Use details from the passage in your description.

Research Navigation

Use the following Web sites to learn more about National Aboriginal Day.

http://www.ainc-inac.gc.ca/nad/hty_e.html

http://www.pch.gc.ca/special/canada/11/index_e.cfm

What are some events people participate in to celebrate June 21?

- Use this Web site for a listing of events.

http://www.ainc-inac.gc.ca/nad/index_e.html

- Go to the Events section and then click on *Ideas for Events*.

- Use the list to plan a day of celebration. Make a schedule of events for your celebration of National Aboriginal Day. Add your own ideas to the schedule.

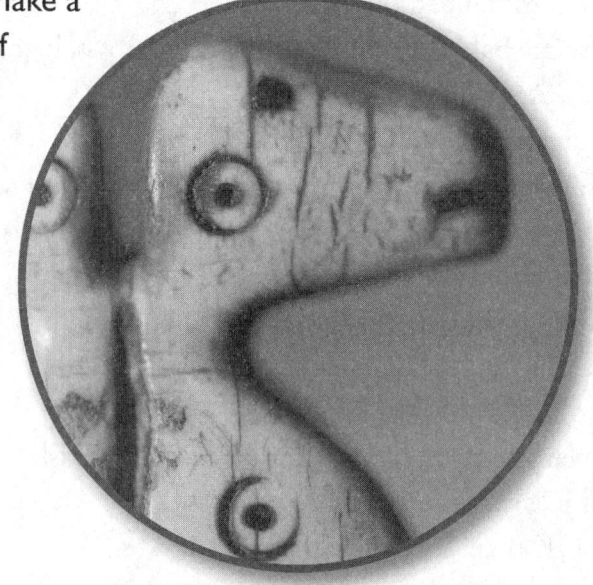

Lesson 9: The Beauty of British Columbia

"I can't wait to get to Okanagan (pronounced *o-ki-NOG-in*) Lake," Bryce said.

"I know you're excited about looking for lake monsters, but we have lots of fun exploring to do before we get to Okanagan," Avaron replied.

"You're right. There's lots of cool stuff to see in British Columbia," Bryce said.

Located on the west coast, the landscape of British Columbia is one of mountains, valleys, rivers, and forests. The kids had just flown into the provincial capital of Victoria, located on Vancouver Island.

"Let's drop our bags at the hostel and go to Beacon Hill Park," Bryce suggested. In the park, the kids strolled past the many ponds and flower gardens. They stopped to watch peacocks that were walking through the rock garden. Then they saw two huge birds flying overhead. They watched as one of the birds landed in its nest.

"Those are bald eagles! I read that there is a pair that nests here," Avaron said.

Bald eagles are found only in North America. They build nests of sticks on cliffs or in isolated trees, close to water. The powerful birds have a wingspan between six and eight feet.

"I think we should do all of British Columbia in a day," said Bryce.

"What are you talking about? Are you in that big of a hurry to get to Okanagan Lake?" Avaron asked.

Bryce laughed. "No, that's how the Royal British Columbia Museum was described in my guidebook," he explained.

"Oh, OK then, let's go to the museum," said Avaron.

As they wandered through the museum, Bryce spotted an exhibit that he had read about. "Check out that hairy elephant," he said.

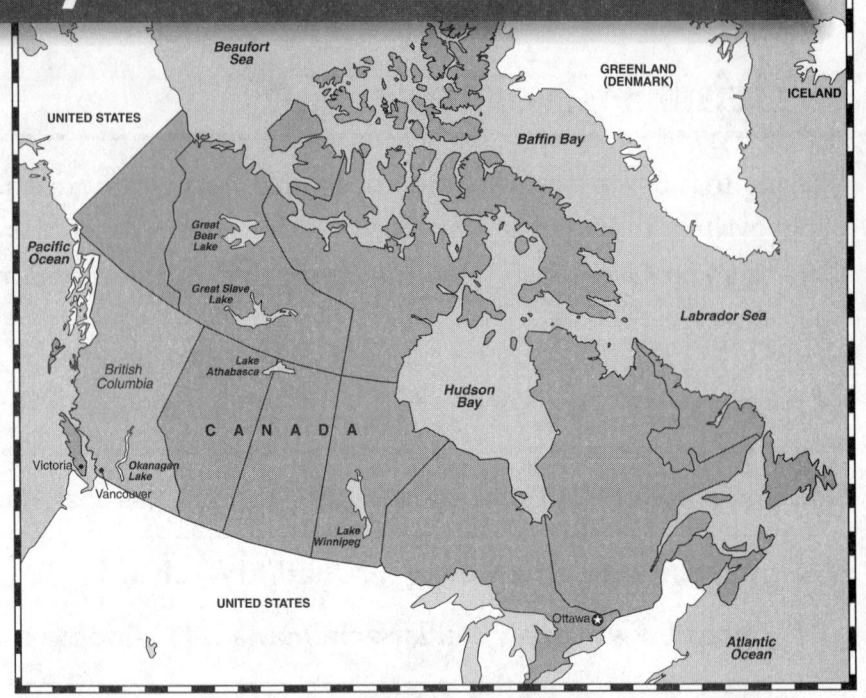

Bald eagles are found throughout North America. British Columbia is home to about 20,000 of these majestic birds.

BRITISH COLUMBIA | CANADA

"Do you mean the woolly mammoth?" Avaron asked.

Bryce laughed. "Yes, it's amazing, isn't it?"

They gazed up at the life-size re-creation of the animal. Extinct for about 17,000 years in British Columbia, the woolly mammoth lived during the last ice age. The museum has over 50 pieces of mammoths. About half of the items were found in British Columbia, mostly on Vancouver Island.

The kids went through the First Peoples Gallery, where they admired carved masks used in ceremonies. They also saw the bags, boxes, and baskets that the people used while gathering food and doing other types of work. They learned some of the ways the First Peoples' cultures changed after contact with Europeans. For example, they saw artifacts made without metal placed next to artifacts made of nothing but metal. They also noticed how artwork changed from showing shamans, or religious leaders, to showing Christian priests.

The next room the kids entered had high ceilings. It was filled with totem poles. The tall posts, made from tree trunks, are covered with carved images. Many of the figures are painted. The totems are symbols. They represent the owner's ancestors as well as both historical and mythical events.

The following day, the kids went to Goldstream Provincial Park. They hiked through the shady woods, passing 600-year-old Douglas fir trees. They sat on moss-covered stones by large waterfalls, feeling the cool mist. They walked along a trail by a river that had observation platforms set up. These were provided for visitors to watch salmon swimming upstream to spawn, or reproduce. The salmon are at their peak from October to December, which attracts bears and eagles who feed on the fish as they make their way back to the place they were born.

"People build fish ladders to help fish that are migrating upstream," Bryce commented.

When a totem pole was erected, many people would carry the pole to a large hole. Then the meanings of the images would be explained. Finally, the pole would be raised and a feast held.

Potlatch

The potlatch is a ceremony observed by the coastal First Nations. During important events, such as the raising of a totem pole, people gather to eat, sing, dance, and receive gifts. The host demonstrates his social status and goodwill by giving gifts.

BRITISH COLUMBIA | CANADA

"I've never heard of a fish ladder. Is this another one of your jokes?" Avaron asked.

Bryce smiled and replied, "No, fish ladders are real things. They've been used for hundreds of years. You'll usually see them by dams. Since the fish can't get past the dam, people make passageways around it. The water washes over a series of steps, and the fish swim and leap up these steps."

"Oooh, gross!" Avaron cried.

"What is gross about a fish ladder?" Bryce asked. He turned to look at Avaron, who was dancing up and down and grimacing. He looked where she was looking.

"Oh, that's a banana slug, the second-largest type of slug in the world," Bryce said. "They can grow as long as nine inches. They eat dead plants and turn them into dirt."

"Well, that's very nice, but I'm getting as far away from that thing as I can," Avaron said.

The following day, the kids rode the ferry to the mainland. They went to Vancouver, Canada's third-largest metropolitan area. Bryce was amazed by the number of people in the city.

"More than half of British Columbia's population lives in Vancouver, Victoria, and other areas of the province's southwestern corner. About 90 percent of Canada's overall population is concentrated within 100 miles of the U.S. border," Avaron said.

They wandered through Stanley Park, one of the world's largest urban parks.

The seawall is a six-mile walkway that looks out on the bay. The walkway is popular with joggers, cyclists, and skaters. The kids passed a statue of a girl in a wet suit, sitting on a rock. They admired a group of large totem poles. They strolled through gardens and across beaches. They tossed crackers to the sea gulls and wood ducks.

"It's amazing that this wide open space is right next to the most densely populated neighborhood in town, the West End," Avaron noted.

"Yeah, if I lived in a residential high-rise, I'd want it to be at the West End. You can escape the big city crowds and noise just by walking into Stanley Park," Bryce said.

People fish for wild salmon. Additionally, salmon are farmed, or raised by humans specifically for food.

Vancouver is considered the primary city of western Canada.

BRITISH COLUMBIA | CANADA

"I'm in the mood for some Chinese food," Avaron said. "Let's have dinner in Chinatown."

Bryce readily agreed. Vancouver's Chinatown is one of the largest in North America, second only to San Francisco's. The kids walked through the bustling open-air market, past baskets of bright pink shrimp, jars of dried herbs, fresh produce, and smelly fish. They had dim sum for dinner. During this multicourse meal, patrons choose what they want from carts that waiters roll by their tables.

The following day, the kids went on a whale-watching tour. Three groups of orcas, also known as killer whales, return to the area each year to feed on salmon. The large mammals, which grow up to 30 feet long, have distinctive black and white markings.

The next morning, the kids traveled to Okanagan Lake. Immediately after arriving, Bryce arranged a boat tour. Many people claim that the lake is the home of the Ogopogo Monster. For over 100 years, there have been sightings of this mysterious snakelike beast. People who have seen it say it is between 15 and 20 feet long and about 2 feet wide.

During the tour, the captain of the boat told them about Ogopogo. "There are stories that the Indians who lived in this area long ago used to carry a small animal with them whenever they traveled on the lake. That way, if the monster surfaced nearby, they could throw the animal in the water and escape while the monster ate it," the captain explained. Bryce scanned the water, and every time he saw something he couldn't identify, he peered through his binoculars and studied it closely.

"Hey, what's that?" he asked excitedly, pointing to the left.

The captain turned the boat in the direction Bryce had indicated. The kids stared at the ripples on the water's surface. Suddenly, they were looking into the eyes of an otter. The animal floated along on its back. The captain laughed.

"Look, there's something over there," Bryce said, pointing to the right.

Again, the captain turned the boat and investigated. They pulled up alongside a large log. Bryce sighed.

"Don't give up yet," the captain said. "I lived here for three years before I saw Ogopogo."

Bryce was amazed. "You've *seen* it?" he asked.

"Yes, I have. But you have to be patient," the captain replied.

Nodding, Bryce raised his binoculars to his eyes again, eagerly scanning the horizon.

Chinatown is an ideal area to experience the culture of China: food, shopping, and the festivals that are held here.

LESSON 9: The Beauty of British Columbia

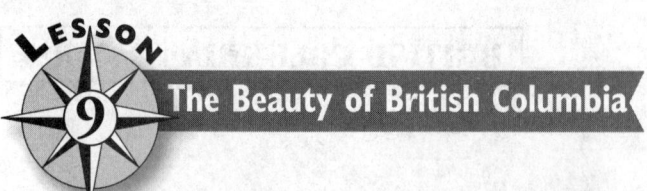

Name _____

Date _____

Chart the Course

Use the table to answer each question.

1. What is the rainiest capital in Canada?
_____

2. Which city gets more snowfall, Winnipeg or Iqaluit?
_____

Which of those two cities gets more rain?
_____

3. Compare the precipitation for Whitehorse and Yellowknife.
_____
_____
_____

Average Precipitation in Canada (inches)

Capitals	Snow	Rain
Regina, Saskatchewan	42	111
Winnipeg, Manitoba	45	159
Edmonton, Alberta	51	137
Toronto, Ontario	53	271
Whitehorse, Yukon Territory	57	62
Yellowknife, Northwest Territories	57	61
Iqaluit, Nunavut	101	76
Halifax, Nova Scotia	102	477
Fredericton, New Brunswick	115	330
St. John's, Newfoundland	126	454
Québec City, Québec	131	344
Charlottetown, Prince Edward Island	132	339
Victoria, British Columbia	189	320

4. What sports might people participate in in Québec?
_____
_____

5. Find the average precipitation for the capital of your state (from the Internet or local weather station). How does it compare with the precipitation in Victoria?
_____
_____
_____

LESSON 9: The Beauty of British Columbia

Name _____

Date _____

Vocabulary Voyage

Write the vocabulary term from the box that matches the definition.

| dense | dim sum | orca | potlatch |
| provincial | totem pole | woolly mammoth | |

1. _____ a selection of small dishes to make a meal

2. _____ a type of whale

3. _____ an extinct elephant with a covering of long hair

4. _____ a post covered with carved and painted symbols

5. _____ a special ceremony of the native peoples of the Pacific Northwest

6. _____ crowded together

7. _____ associated with or relating to a province

Use each vocabulary term from the box to write a complete sentence of your own.

_____
_____
_____
_____
_____
_____
_____
_____

LESSON 9: The Beauty of British Columbia

Name _____

Date _____

Comprehension Expedition

Darken the circle for the best answer.

1. What occupied Vancouver Island in prehistoric times?
   - Ⓐ Orcas
   - Ⓑ Mammoths
   - Ⓒ First People
   - Ⓓ Europeans

2. How do you know there was Chinese immigration to western Canada?
   - Ⓐ Parts of Vancouver are densely populated.
   - Ⓑ There is a large Chinatown in Vancouver.
   - Ⓒ Salmon fishing is important in the area.
   - Ⓓ Population is concentrated near the U.S. border.

3. What evidence in this passage supports the following statement?
   Salmon fishing is an important industry in British Columbia.
   - Ⓐ People keep banana slugs near salmon streams.
   - Ⓑ People build parks to watch salmon climb ladders.
   - Ⓒ People build dams to stop salmon from migrating.
   - Ⓓ People build fish ladders to help fish migrate upstream.

Use complete sentences to answer the question.

4. What did Europeans introduce to the First Peoples in British Columbia?

_____
_____
_____
_____
_____
_____
_____

Lesson 9: The Beauty of British Columbia

Name _____

Date _____

Writing Adventure

Imagine that Bryce and Avaron suddenly spot something unidentifiable in the waters of Okanagan Lake. Is it Ogopogo? What will the captain do when he sees it? Write a story that tells what happens. Include a description of what the kids see and how all the tourists on the boat react.

Research Navigation

Follow these steps and answer the questions as you go.

- Go to the Internet Web site for The Canadian Encyclopedia.

  http://www.thecanadianencyclopedia.com/

- Why are there two language choices on the homepage?

- Click on *English*. Click on *Interactive Resources*. Find *Interactive Maps*. Click on *Canada's Native Peoples*.

- What do you hear when the map comes on-screen?

- Explore the map by clicking on different regions to learn about Canada's native peoples.

- Write two things you learned about the native peoples of the Northwest Coast.

LESSON 10
Yukon Territory: Gold Rush

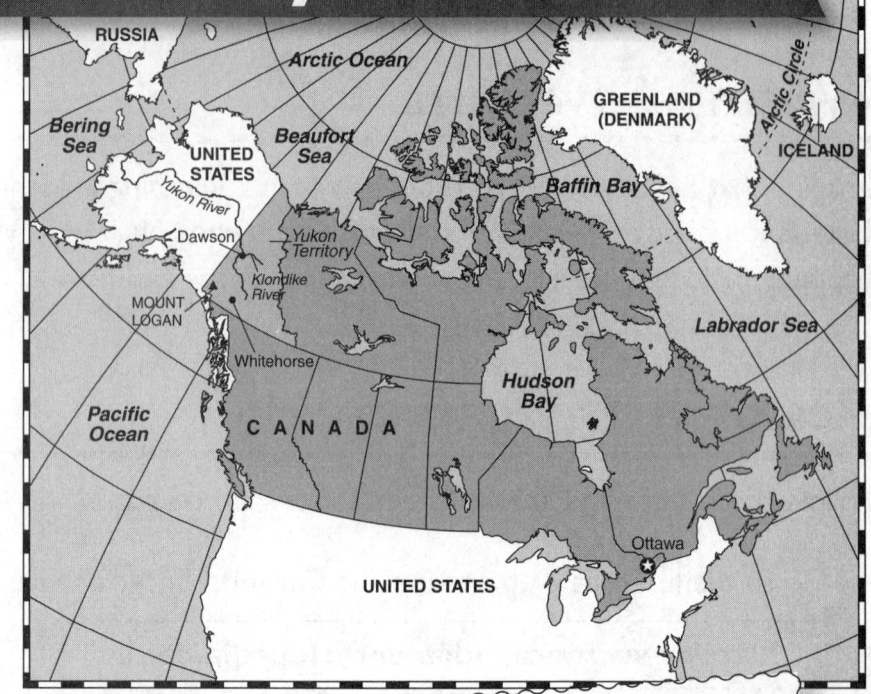

"Well, we're not in the Northwest Territories, but we are in the northwestern corner of Canada," Bryce said.

"Yeah, it's funny how names of places can be misleading," Avaron replied.

The kids had just flown into Whitehorse, the capital of the Yukon Territory. Located north of British Columbia, the Yukon shares its western border with Alaska and its eastern border with the Northwest Territories. Although the summer here is warm, it is short. Winter, on the other hand, is cold and long. Because the Yukon is located so far north, summer days last almost 20 hours, while winter days last about 5 hours. This is due to the way Earth tilts toward the sun during the summer and away from it during winter.

More than 2,000 miles long, the Yukon River starts on the border of the Yukon Territory and British Columbia. It flows northwestward, crossing Alaska all the way to the Arctic Circle. Here, it changes direction, flowing southwestward into the Bering Sea. Whitehorse is one of the chief ports on the river.

The Yukon River near Whitehorse

"One of the Yukon River's main tributaries, or streams, is the Klondike River. In 1896, the discovery of gold along the Klondike made worldwide headlines," said Bryce.

YUKON TERRITORY | CANADA

"Tens of thousands of people made the journey to Dawson, where the gold had been found. It took 6 months to travel into the wilderness," Avaron noted.

Many prospectors started on their search for gold in Dyea, Alaska. They hiked the Chilkoot Trail, located south of Whitehorse. When they got to the Yukon River, they had to build boats for the remainder of the journey. They finally arrived in Dawson, after a 500-mile journey.

The trip was very difficult and dangerous. Prospectors endured harsh winter months with 60-mile-per-hour winds and temperatures as low as 65 degrees below zero. The harsh weather often caused ice and snow to crash down a mountain. Prospectors were faced with the dangers of these avalanches, as well as blinding snow, accidents, and illness. It took some prospectors 2 weeks to travel 10 miles. Some people lost their belongings as soon as they arrived on the mudflats at Dyea. When the tide came in, it flooded the beach and washed away their supplies.

Prospectors had to purchase supplies.

Due to shortages caused by the large numbers of people entering the territory and using everything up, prospectors were required to carry a ton of supplies. This one-year supply of provisions included food, tools, and clothing. Goods were checked by Mounties, the Canadian police force, before the prospectors were allowed entry into Canada. It took about 40 trips to carry the supplies up the narrow, slick, rough trail to Chilkoot Pass.

The town of Dawson was originally a summer fish camp. During one week of the gold rush, the population grew from 500 to 12,000 people. By the end of the summer of 1898, there were 30,000 people in Dawson. However, the gold rush was short-lived, ending in 1898. Dawson's current population is about 2,000 people.

The current population of Whitehorse, the largest city in the Yukon Territory, is about 20,000 people. There are only about 30,000 people in the entire territory.

"Maybe they should rename the province and call it The Big Empty," Bryce mused.

The kids had arranged to hike the 33-mile Chilkoot Trail with a small tour group. They were driven across the border and into Alaska, where they began hiking in the ghost town of Dyea. The trail went through Alaska, British Columbia, and into the Yukon Territory.

YUKON TERRITORY | CANADA

For four days, the group walked along the trail, through bogs, up and down mountains, and past graves of the prospectors who didn't make it to the gold fields. They saw evidence of human life many years before. Artifacts including wagon wheels, rusty shovels, rotten boots, and broken bottles were scattered along the way.

At trail's end, a bus took the kids back to their bed-and-breakfast in Whitehorse. Bryce said, "That was amazing and beautiful and fun, but I'm exhausted. I can't believe so many thousands of people completed that hike, carrying a ton of supplies, only to have to build boats and endure the rapids and wildlife along the Yukon River."

"And most of them never even found any gold after arriving in Dawson!" Avaron commented.

Bryce stayed in the room to rest while Avaron went out to explore the town. When she returned, she suggested they go eat dinner before the evening's entertainment.

"What entertainment? I'm tired. I don't really feel like getting any more exercise right now," Bryce complained.

"Oh, come on, I think you'll like it. Besides, all you have to do is sit down and hold on," Avaron replied.

After eating, Bryce followed Avaron outside, where she sat on a bench outside the restaurant.

"What are you doing? Is this your evening entertainment?" Bryce asked.

"Yeah, how do you like it?" Avaron replied, grinning.

"Uh, well, it's pretty relaxing, but a little bit boring," Bryce said.

A car pulled up and stopped. Avaron got up and walked toward it. Puzzled, Bryce followed her.

After they were seated, the driver said, "So, are you ready for your ride?"

"Ride? What kind of ride?" Bryce asked. The driver looked at Avaron, and she and Avaron laughed as the car moved down the road.

A few minutes later, the car turned down a long dirt driveway. Bryce heard howling and barking. He peered out the window, trying to figure out where they

A Mountie in uniform

Mounties

The North West Mounted Police (NWMP) was a Canadian police force created in 1873. When miners from the U.S. began pouring across the border to look for gold, the NWMP collected fees on goods taken in and out of the country. In addition to collecting customs duties, Mounties enforced Canadian law. They were so successful in maintaining peace and order that they became world famous. Eventually renamed the Royal Canadian Mounted Police, this federal police force is still active today.

YUKON TERRITORY | CANADA

were going. Then he saw dozens of huskies. A man was putting several of the dogs in harness.

"Wow, are we going dog-sledding? I didn't think that was possible during the summer!" Bryce exclaimed.

"We run the dogs to keep them in shape," Shelly, the driver and head musher, explained. "During the winter, I drive a team of dogs in races and sometimes to haul supplies. During the summer, when there is no snow, we harness them to a wheeled buggy. Your sister has arranged for you both to come along for the ride tonight."

"This is great! Huskies are my favorite dogs!" said Bryce.

A team of 12 huskies was hooked up to the buggy. The dogs were very excited and ready to run. The kids piled in, along with Shelly. She explained that dog teams are controlled by nothing more than voice commands. There are no reins or leashes.

The command "gee" tells the dogs to turn right, while "haw" tells them to turn left. When the musher, or dog team driver, says "hike," the dogs know to run fast.

After an exhilarating ride, the kids returned to their room. They got a good night's sleep, even though it was still light outside when they went to bed. The next morning, they took a bus to Kluane National Park.

"Look, there's Mount Logan, Canada's highest mountain," Bryce said, pointing at the 19,545-foot peak.

The kids spent two days exploring the vast park's mountains, glaciers, marshes, and sand dunes. They heard wolves howling at night, and they watched a herd of caribou travel across an open field. They also saw a grizzly bear feasting on berries.

"Grizzlies can grow up to 8 feet long and weigh as much as 900 pounds," Avaron noted.

"It's such an honor to see these animals in the wild. I'm just glad she's more interested in eating berries than us," Bryce laughed.

A well-trained team of sled dogs can average about 20 miles per hour.

Canada has a large population of grizzly bears.

81

www.harcourtschoolsupply.com
© Harcourt Achieve Inc. All rights reserved.

Canada: Lesson 10
Journeys Around the World, SV 1419027875

LESSON 10

Yukon Territory: Gold Rush

Name

Date

Map Exploration

Use an atlas or Internet map site to complete the map of Canada.

1. Mark the provinces of Québec, Manitoba, British Columbia, Yukon Territory, and Northwest Territories on the map.

2. Add the capital of Canada to the map.

3. Put the following cities on the map: Montréal, Victoria, Winnipeg, St. John's.

4. Label the bodies of water that border Canada on the north.

5. Label the country to the south.

Lesson 10: Yukon Territory: Gold Rush

Name _____
Date _____

Vocabulary Voyage

Use the context clues from the passage as a definition. Write the vocabulary term from the box that goes with the correct context clue.

| artifacts | avalanche | customs duties | harsh | musher |
| prospector | provisions | tributaries | shortage | |

1. ... ice and snow to crash down a mountain _____
2. ... winter months with 60-mile-per-hour winds and temperatures as low as 65 degrees below zero _____
3. ... search for gold ... _____
4. ... fees on goods taken in and out of the country _____
5. supplies ... included food, tools, and clothing _____
6. ... evidence of human ... including wagon wheels, rusty shovels, rotten boots, and broken bottles ... _____
7. using everything up ... _____
8. ... drive a team of dogs ... _____
9. ... streams ... _____

Use each vocabulary term from the box to write a complete sentence of your own.

_____
_____
_____
_____
_____
_____
_____
_____

LESSON 10 — Yukon Territory: Gold Rush

Name _____

Date _____

Comprehension Expedition

Darken the circle for the best answer.

1. Why was it still light outside when the kids went to bed in the Yukon Territory?
   - Ⓐ There is nothing to do at night, so everyone goes to bed early.
   - Ⓑ There are only a few hours of darkness at night in the winter.
   - Ⓒ There are only a few hours of darkness at night in the summer.
   - Ⓓ There are no trees to block the sun in the Arctic region.

2. Why did prospectors endure such terrible conditions when traveling?
   - Ⓐ They each wanted to be the first person to explore the area.
   - Ⓑ They had no idea what they were getting into.
   - Ⓒ They were special people who didn't mind the hardship.
   - Ⓓ They had hopes of striking gold and getting very rich.

3. Why did the population of Dawson probably decrease from 30,000 to 2,000?
   - Ⓐ There was terrible weather.
   - Ⓑ There wasn't any more gold to find.
   - Ⓒ There weren't any more dog sleds.
   - Ⓓ There weren't any more fish to catch.

Use complete sentences to answer the question.

4. How do you know sled dogs are well trained?

_____
_____
_____
_____
_____
_____
_____
_____

Yukon Territory: Gold Rush

Name _____
Date _____

Writing Adventure

Imagine you are heading to the Yukon Territory today and must bring a one-year supply of provisions with you. What will you bring? Make a list. Compare your list with a friend's. Write a statement about why you chose to bring one item that your friend did not.

Research Navigation

This lesson completes Bryce and Avaron's trip to Canada. Imagine that you are going to take a trip to Canada, but you can visit only three places. Use the Internet, travel guides, and reference books to pick the three places you would like to see. Plot your trip on a map and make a schedule of where you will visit and what modes of transportation you'll use. Compile your information into a trip itinerary folder.

Lesson 11: A City Without a State

"Washington, D.C., is the only city in the U.S. that isn't in a state," Bryce noted.

"It's also one of the few cities in the nation that was designed before it was built," said Avaron.

"And we really benefit from that, with all of these majestic buildings and monuments to explore," said Bryce.

"Not to mention the large lawns, old trees, and reflecting pools," Avaron added.

The District of Columbia (the *D.C.* in *Washington, D.C.*) was named by Congress in honor of Christopher Columbus. The land was donated by Virginia and Maryland, and Washington, D.C., became the official capital of the United States in 1800.

"A capital is a city that serves as the seat of government. A capitol is the building in which the functions of a government are carried out. What if we start our tour in the capital's Capitol?" Avaron asked.

The Capitol is where both the House of Representatives and the Senate meet. Together, they are called Congress. The kids and a group of other visitors toured the rooms where these legislators work to make laws.

The tour guide explained, "The Constitution provides for a separation of powers. The three branches of government are legislative, judicial, and executive. They work together, but they are separate from one another. Each branch can check the power of the others in order to maintain a balance of power."

Avaron asked, "What happens if Congress passes a bill that the president disagrees with?"

"This is where the three branches come in," the tour guide explained. "The president, who is part of the executive branch, can veto a bill. This stops a bill from becoming a law. The Supreme Court, or judicial branch, can declare a law or an action by the president unconstitutional. Congress, the legislative branch, can impeach, or remove from office, the president or the Supreme Court justices."

Government buildings form a dramatic skyline in Washington, D.C.

WASHINGTON, D.C. | UNITED STATES

"I see what they mean by a balanced government," said Bryce.

The kids' next stop was the nearby Supreme Court building. The Supreme Court is the highest court in the country. Its nine justices are appointed for life. They come together on the first Monday each October and stay in session until all cases have been heard and decisions have been handed down on all of them.

"These buildings are so big and grand. I feel almost like I'm on a movie set," Bryce mused.

"Yeah, the architecture is amazing," Avaron agreed. "And just think how much history occurred here. It's awe-inspiring!"

The kids walked down the National Mall, a two-mile strip of land covered with marble buildings, pools, fountains, and wide green lawns.

As they strolled past the many museums, Avaron said, "We could spend a few weeks here and still not see everything in these museums. I guess we'll need to do some research to try to figure out what we want to see most."

"I know I want to see at least one thing in the National Museum of American History," said Bryce. "We can't leave until we see George Washington's wooden teeth!"

"That's a myth. His false teeth were made of gold, ivory, lead, and other teeth. The museum also has a special watch used by Helen Keller," explained Avaron.

"Cool!" Bryce responded. "I've heard of that touch watch. Since Helen Keller couldn't see, she could 'read' the watch by touching it. Let's put the National Museum of American History on our list of things we must do."

Avaron suggested they stop at the National Archive. It contains about five billion documents. The Declaration of Independence, the Constitution, and the Bill of Rights are considered the country's most important papers. The kids were able to view these documents displayed in airtight cases.

"Each night, these documents are lowered into a 50-ton vault that is 20 feet underground for safekeeping. And the building is fireproof," Bryce noted.

"I'm glad to know the papers that formed our government are kept safe!" Avaron said.

"The American colonies declared their independence from the British in 1776," Bryce commented.

How a Law Is Passed

The basic lawmaking process has many steps. A bill might get started when people contact their representative with an idea that they believe should be a law. If the representative agrees, he or she writes a bill and introduces it in Congress. Representatives discuss the bill, and if the report is favorable, the bill is voted on by the House of Representatives. If it is passed here, it proceeds to the Senate, where the process is repeated. If the Senate passes the bill, it goes to the president. The president either signs it into law or vetoes it.

Above the 16 marble columns at the front entrance of the Supreme Court building are the words "Equal Justice under Law."

WASHINGTON, D.C. | UNITED STATES

"And the U.S. Constitution was written in 1787," said Avaron.

"The Bill of Rights was written two years later," Bryce added.

"That was certainly a busy time for our country," Avaron noted.

The kids proceeded to the White House.

"So this is where the president lives. Did you know the White House has its own zip code?" Bryce asked.

"It also has a tennis court, swimming pool, movie theater, bowling lane, jogging track, and a game room with table tennis and pool tables," Avaron replied.

"That doesn't sound like such a bad place to live," Bryce laughed.

"Of course, it also houses all the presidential offices, including the famous Oval Office," added Avaron.

"The president doesn't have a long commute to work!" laughed Bryce.

Their next stop was the Washington Monument. Towering 555 feet, it is the tallest monument in the city. This simple marble pillar has a square base and a pointed top. The kids rode the elevator to the observation room at the summit. Avaron pointed out the cherry trees south of the monument. She told Bryce that over 3,000 of the trees were given to the U.S. as gifts by Japan in 1912.

As the kids walked toward the Jefferson Memorial, Bryce yawned and stretched. "I probably shouldn't admit this, but I'm getting a little bit tired of monuments. Maybe we should stop and eat."

"We can eat soon. I think you're going to like a sculpture I read about that's close to the Jefferson Memorial," Avaron replied.

The kids arrived at a five-part sculpture that shows a 100-foot-tall man who is half-buried. Called *The Awakening*, the sculpture shows a screaming head, an arm, a hand, a knee, and a foot, so it looks as if the man is trying to break out of the ground.

Bryce crawled into the giant's mouth while Avaron took photos. Then she posed, peeking through the giant's fingers. She also stood by the giant's foot and held her nose, while Bryce laughed.

"You're right. I love this sculpture. It's my favorite site so far today, and there have been lots of amazing sites," Bryce said.

The kids ate and rested for a while before returning to the National Mall. At its western end they saw the Vietnam Veterans Memorial. The black granite wall is inscribed with the names of the more than 58,000 people

The Bill of Rights

The first ten amendments to the Constitution are known as the Bill of Rights. They ensure basic liberties such as freedom of speech, freedom of religion, protection from unreasonable searches or seizures, and the right to a speedy and public trial.

The White House is open to the public, free of charge.

The Washington Monument

WASHINGTON, D.C. | UNITED STATES

who were killed or who are missing. They saw the mementos people had left at the wall, including flowers, small flags, photographs, and letters.

"Another thing I want to put on our list of things to see in the museums is the collection of mementos that have been gathered from this monument over the years. On a typical day, between 10 and 20 items are left. On holidays such as Memorial Day, as many as 1,000 items are left," Avaron said.

"I'd really like to see that, too," Bryce agreed. "I read that the first item left here actually became part of the memorial. When the concrete for the foundation was being poured, a Navy officer tossed his dead brother's Purple Heart in the concrete. The officer said he wanted to give it to the Wall."

The kids' final stop for the day was at the Lincoln Memorial. This famous monument is depicted on both the penny and the five-dollar bill. Its 36 columns represent each of the states that were in existence at the time of Lincoln's death. A large statue of the sixteenth president sitting in a chair is inside the building.

"That statue of Lincoln is huge and commanding," said Bryce. "Did you know that this was where Martin Luther King, Jr., gave his 'I Have a Dream' speech? So many amazing things have happened in this city."

Exhausted, the kids took the bus back to the hostel and began planning their activities for the following day. Avaron wanted to go to the Library of Congress, which is the largest library in the world. It has millions of books, and many architectural experts claim that it is the city's most beautiful building. Bryce wanted to go by the F.B.I. headquarters, as well as the Bureau of Engraving and Printing, where they could watch money being printed.

"Let's also go to Arlington National Cemetery. More than a quarter million veterans, from every war the U.S. has fought, are buried there," Avaron said.

"And that's located close to the Pentagon, the headquarters for the U.S. Armed Forces," Bryce said. "Maybe we could fit that in as well."

"It's going to be another busy day, that's for sure," Avaron replied.

The Vietnam Veterans Memorial

The 19-foot statue of Lincoln faces the Washington Monument and the Capitol building.

LESSON 11
A City Without a State

Name _____
Date _____

Map Exploration

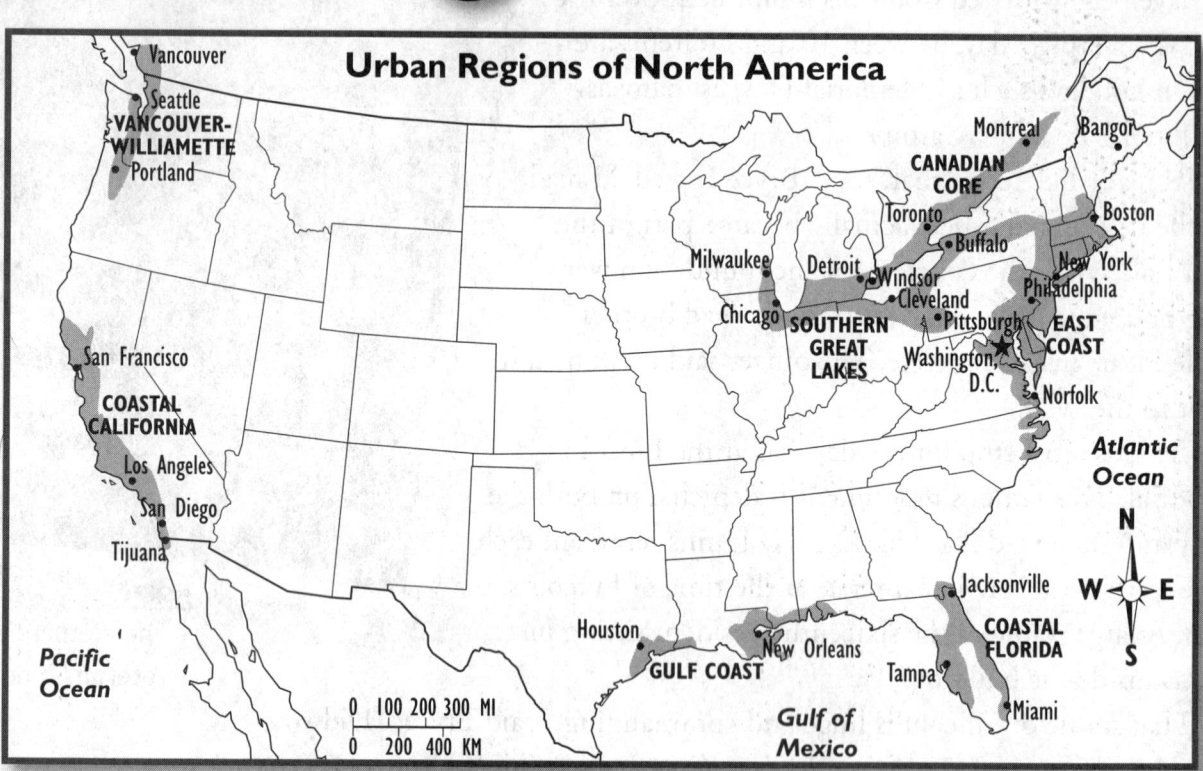

Urban Regions of North America

Use the map to answer the questions.

1. In what urban region is Washington, D.C., found? _____

2. What urban region lies north of the Great Lakes? _____

3. What cities make up the Coastal California region? _____
_____

4. What do the cities in Coastal Florida, the Gulf Coast, and Coastal California have in common?
_____

5. What do all the urban regions have in common? _____

Why might so many people want to live in these areas? _____

Lesson 11: A City Without a State

Name _____

Date _____

Vocabulary Voyage

Write the word from the box that matches the definition. Then use the numbered letters to complete the sentence.

capital	executive	Congress	capitol	impeach
judicial	legislative	legislators	veto	

1. lawmakers __ __ __ __ __ __ __ __ __ __
             4   9

2. the location of a government __ __ __ __ __ __ __
                            7

3. to remove an elected official from office because of unlawful behavior
   __ __ __ __ __ __ __
     6

4. the president, vice president, and Cabinet make up this branch of government
   __ __ __ __ __ __ __ __ __
            8

5. the House of Representatives and the Senate and other government agencies make up this branch of government __ __ __ __ __ __ __ __ __ __ __
                     3

6. the building where the legislature meets __ __ __ __ __ __ __
                                    10

7. the main lawmaking body, made up of the House of Representatives and the Senate
   __ __ __ __ __ __ __ __
     2 11

8. the power of the president to stop a bill from becoming a law __ __ __ __
                        5

9. the Supreme Court and other federal courts make up this branch of government
   __ __ __ __ __ __ __ __
     1

In 1814, during the War of 1812, British troops set fire to the White House. First Lady

__ __ __ __ __ y __ __ d __ __ __ __ packed many valuables,
1 2 3 4 5   6 7   8 9 10 11

including a portrait of George Washington, and saved them from the fire.

LESSON 11: A City Without a State

Name _____

Date _____

Comprehension Expedition

Darken the circle for the best answer.

1. What is the last step a federal law goes through?
   - Ⓐ It goes to the president to be signed or vetoed.
   - Ⓑ It goes to the Senate for approval.
   - Ⓒ It goes the House of Representatives to be voted on.
   - Ⓓ It goes to the Congress to be signed or vetoed.

2. Which of these is NOT protected by the Bill of Rights?
   - Ⓐ Right to freedom of speech
   - Ⓑ Right to practice any religion
   - Ⓒ Right to good education
   - Ⓓ Right to a public trial

3. Why is the Supreme Court important?
   - Ⓐ It solves only important cases.
   - Ⓑ It can declare a passed law invalid.
   - Ⓒ It can impeach the president.
   - Ⓓ It signs all laws.

Use complete sentences to answer the question.

4. How do the branches of government make sure that one branch does not become too powerful? Provide examples.

_____
_____
_____
_____
_____
_____
_____
_____

LESSON 11: A City Without a State

Name

Date

Writing Adventure

Imagine that you are on a tour of the White House and are separated from your group. You wander around the building until you realize it is late and all the tours are over. There's a tap on your shoulder, and you turn around and are face to face with the President of the United States. Write a story about what happens.

Research Navigation

In addition to soldiers, some Supreme Court justices, astronauts, and explorers are buried at Arlington National Cemetery. Two presidents are buried there also.

- Go to the following Web site to find which two presidents are buried at Arlington National Cemetery.

    http://www.arlingtoncemetery.org/

- Who at Arlington National Cemetery has an eternal flame on his grave?

LESSON 12: Exploring the Deep South: Alabama

"The people here sure are friendly," Bryce commented.

"Yeah, Southern hospitality is wonderful. I feel very welcome here," Avaron replied.

The kids were at Vulcan Park in Birmingham, Alabama. They stared up at the world's largest cast-iron statue, which overlooks the city. The statue is Vulcan, the Roman god of fire, iron, and metalworking. He became a symbol for Birmingham's industry. The 56-foot-tall statue stands on a 124-foot base. The kids went to the top of the observation tower and looked out at the view.

Birmingham is the largest city in Alabama, and it is nicknamed the Magic City. It got this name because of its rapid growth after being founded in 1871. Rich in minerals such as iron ore, coal, and limestone, the city was a major steel-producing center for over a century.

"Look at all of the amazing, lush vines growing all over the hillsides," Avaron said.

"Yeah, they seem to cover everything. I wonder what that plant is," Bryce replied.

A woman who was standing nearby overheard Bryce and Avaron. "That vine is called kudzu," she explained. "I've lived in Alabama all my life. I've been forced to deal with the fast-growing plant because it grows on my property. Even though it's difficult to control, I love it for its beauty."

Kudzu grows quickly and can cover lampposts, trees, and even buildings.

After learning about kudzu, Bryce asked the woman if she would recommend a nearby restaurant that served good Southern food. She gave the kids directions to a place near UAB, the University of Alabama at Birmingham. This college's nationally recognized medical center has six health-related schools, including the School of Medicine, the School of Nursing, and the School of Dentistry.

"I guess if we were to have any health problems, we'd be in the right place," Avaron commented.

The kids ate fried chicken, mashed potatoes with gravy, green beans, and pecan pie.

"Now *that* was a meal! No wonder nobody wants to leave this state," said Bryce.

Most people born in Alabama live there throughout their lives. The state has the largest native-born population in the country. Almost three-quarters of its residents are natives.

The kids rode a bus to the Civil Rights Institute, located downtown. They entered a small theater and watched a short movie. The movie ended with a scene showing segregated water fountains. One was marked "White," and the other was marked "Colored." The movie screen rose into the ceiling, and there were the same two water fountains attached to a wall. The kids walked past them and saw displays of people in a variety of activities. One showed people holding a sit-in at a restaurant counter. People sat at the counter and refused to move until they were served. Nearby, the kids read how this and other forms of civil disobedience were used in the fight for equal rights.

"It's hard to believe that there was a time in our country when people were refused service based on the color of their skin," said Avaron.

"I sure am glad so much has changed and improved over the years," Bryce commented.

As they continued their tour of the museum, the kids learned how people once used violence and fear to support segregation. In 1954, the Supreme Court ruled that public schools could not be segregated. The court said that keeping a group of people separate from the rest of the population was not the way to achieve equality. There was fierce resistance to this ruling by those who wanted the races to stay separated. However, progress continued to march forward.

The kids read information about laws that were passed to address racial injustice. These included the Civil Rights Act of 1964 and the Voting Rights Act of 1965. After seeing all of the displays, the kids walked outside to Kelly Ingram Park. The park had been used for civil rights demonstrations during the 1960s.

Kudzu

Known as the foot-a-day plant due to its amazing growth during the summer months, kudzu covers millions of acres in the South. However, it is not a native plant. It was brought from Japan in the nineteenth century. During the 1930s, the government encouraged its use because it helped prevent soil erosion. However, it was later labeled a harmful weed because it damages its surroundings.

ALABAMA | UNITED STATES

The following day, the kids took a bus to Montgomery, Alabama's capital. Their first stop was the Rosa Parks Museum. This museum stands on the corner where a simple act of civil disobedience helped to change the course of segregation in the U.S. The museum provides information about Parks's life, the Montgomery bus boycott, and the civil rights movement.

On December 1, 1955, Rosa Parks, a black woman, was riding the bus home from work. The seats in the front of the bus were reserved for whites, while the seats at the back of the bus were for blacks. The front section was full, and when a white man got on the bus, the driver told Mrs. Parks to give the man her seat. She refused. After her arrest, the African-American community organized a boycott of the bus line. They continued this boycott, or refusal to ride public buses, as a way to protest the unfair bus service. The community formed the Montgomery Improvement Association, and Martin Luther King, Jr., was chosen as its president. Eventually, the Supreme Court ruled that the segregated service was against the law. Rosa Parks's simple act of not giving up her seat had a major impact on the civil rights movement.

The kids' next stop was Tuskegee, located about 35 miles east of Montgomery. Here, they visited Tuskegee (pronounced *tus-KEE-gee*) University. Originally a school for African-American teachers, it was founded by Booker T. Washington in 1881. Washington was an educator and reformer who realized how important education was for African Americans during the post-Reconstruction period.

"This is where George Washington Carver worked," Bryce said. "He was an important agricultural chemist who headed the school's agriculture department. He also conducted most of his research here."

"Yeah, I read that he was responsible for important improvements in agriculture. He knew that the soil had been exhausted by farmers who had planted nothing but cotton, so he encouraged them to plant peanuts and

When Rosa Parks refused to give up her seat on a bus, she changed history.

Martin Luther King, Jr.

Martin Luther King, Jr., was one of America's great leaders. He led the civil rights movement during the 1950s and 1960s with peaceful protests. He helped bring about major social change. King received the Nobel Peace Prize in 1964. He was assassinated in 1968.

soybeans. These crops provided a source of protein and also helped the soil to recover. He helped to make both peanut and sweet potato crops profitable by developing other products from them. For example, he learned how to make ink, plastics, and soap from peanuts. And he made flour, rubber, and postage stamp glue from sweet potatoes," Avaron commented.

"When the school started, it had one room. It grew and changed over the years, becoming a university in 1985. Today, it has over 100 buildings. It is well known for its science and engineering programs," Bryce noted.

The kids' final stop was Mobile. Located on Mobile Bay on the Gulf of Mexico, it is an important port city. Filled with towering, centuries-old oak trees, its streets are lined with large, stately homes.

The kids toured Magnolia Cemetery, one of Mobile's oldest burial grounds. The cemetery was established in 1825. It was needed at that time because yellow fever was killing many people. Yellow fever is a serious disease that is spread by mosquitoes. The United States is now free of the disease.

"There are so many beautiful tombstones and statues here. It's a very peaceful place," Avaron commented.

The children explored the cemetery for a few hours, finding graves of Confederate soldiers, statues of dogs, and a mysterious iron statue of an unknown woman. As they walked out the gate in the late afternoon, they saw a group of black kids and white kids playing soccer in a nearby park.

"Alabama seceded from the nation at the beginning of the Civil War. I sure am glad the state rejoined the union. This is a cool place," Bryce mused.

Avaron smiled and nodded in agreement.

George Washington Carver

A headstone in historic Magnolia Cemetery

LESSON 12
Exploring the Deep South: Alabama

Name _____

Date _____

Map Exploration

Civil War Divides the States

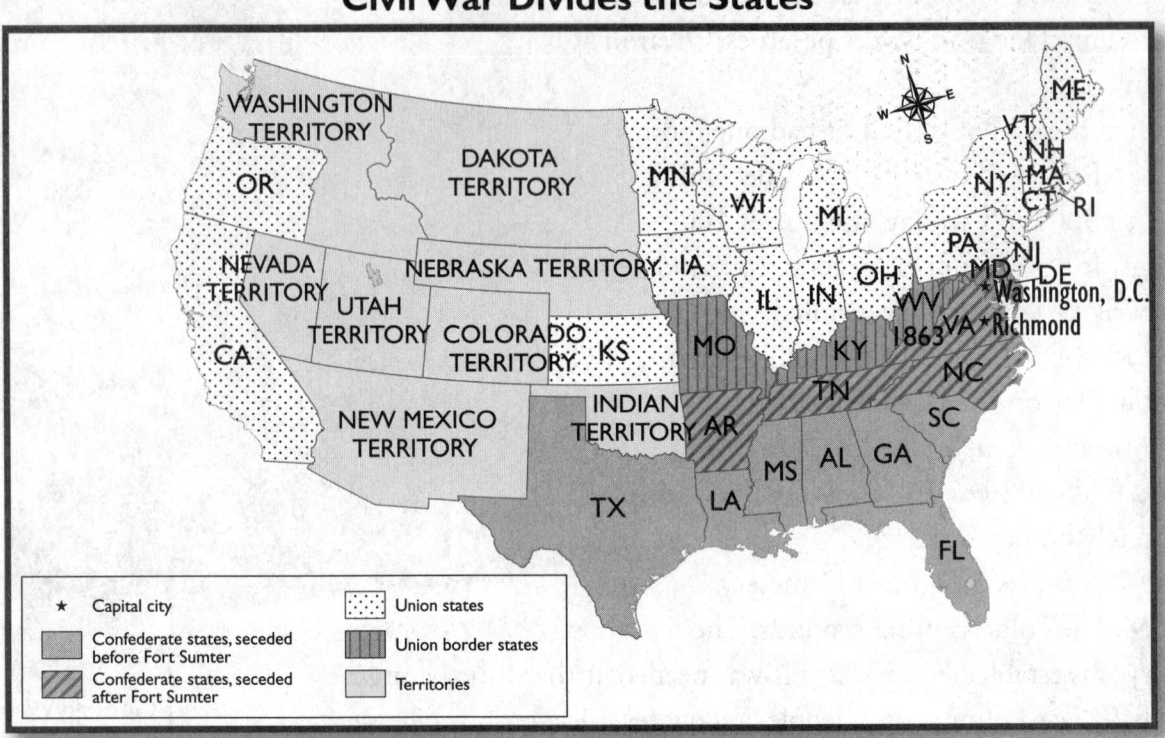

Legend:
- ★ Capital city
- Confederate states, seceded before Fort Sumter
- Confederate states, seceded after Fort Sumter
- Union states
- Union border states
- Territories

Use the map to answer the questions.

1. What states seceded from the country at the same time as Alabama?

_____

2. How was Richmond important during the Civil War?

_____

3. What Union states bordered Alabama?

_____

4. Why might the Union army have wanted to take over Alabama in order to win the war?

_____

5. What was the largest of the Confederate states?

_____

www.harcourtschoolsupply.com
© Harcourt Achieve Inc. All rights reserved.

98

United States: Lesson 12
Journeys Around the World, SV 1419027875

LESSON 12
Exploring the Deep South: Alabama

Name _____

Date _____

Vocabulary Voyage

Write the vocabulary term that goes with the speaker's statement. Use the vocabulary terms in the box.

| boycott | civil disobedience | equality | kudzu |
| resistance | seceded | segregated | sit-in |

1. "I can't see that street sign because it is covered by a big vine." _____

2. "Tomorrow we will fill all the seats in that restaurant, and we won't get up until they serve *all* people." _____

3. "The Confederate states pulled away from the Union and tried to form their own country." _____

4. "This place had separate schools for black children and for white children." _____

5. "Everyone, no matter who they are, deserves the same treatment." _____

6. "I do not approve of their rules, so I refuse to take part in that activity." _____

7. "You can show that you do not agree by acting in a violent way or in a peaceful way." _____

8. "We will not obey that law, but we will do so in a peaceful way. By doing this, we will get the government to change the law." _____

LESSON 12
Exploring the Deep South: Alabama

Name _____

Date _____

Comprehension Expedition

Darken the circle for the best answer.

1. Why was Vulcan chosen as a symbol for Birmingham?
   - Ⓐ He was the god of magic, and Birmingham was nicknamed the Magic City because of its fast growth.
   - Ⓑ He was a Roman god that was a symbol for the Confederate states during the Civil War.
   - Ⓒ He was the god of fire, and Birmingham had violent conflicts during the civil rights movement.
   - Ⓓ He was the god of metalworking, and Birmingham's major industry was steel production.

2. What did Rosa Parks choose as her method to change an unfair law?
   - Ⓐ Civil disobedience
   - Ⓑ Segregation
   - Ⓒ Secession
   - Ⓓ Violent resistance

3. How did George Washington Carver's inventions of ways to make ink and plastics from peanuts change farming methods?
   - Ⓐ His inventions made consumers buy fewer peanuts, which made farmers plant fewer. This increased the growing of cotton.
   - Ⓑ His inventions created a demand for peanuts, which made farmers plant more. The changing of crops saved the soil.
   - Ⓒ His inventions made ink and plastics inexpensive, which made more people buy these products. Many people left farming to work in manufacturing.
   - Ⓓ His inventions created a demand for peanuts, which made farmers plant more. The growing of peanuts contributed to soil exhaustion.

Use complete sentences to answer the question.

4. How did the Supreme Court affect lives in Alabama?

   _____
   _____
   _____
   _____

LESSON 12: Exploring the Deep South: Alabama

Name _____

Date _____

Writing Adventure

The first paragraph of a newspaper story tries to answer the five Ws plus H: *who, what, where, when, why,* and *how.* Imagine that you were a reporter for a newspaper in Montgomery, Alabama, and you are to write a story on Rosa Parks's arrest. Write the first paragraph of your story. Try to cover as many of the five Ws plus H as you can.

Research Navigation

Many well-known people are from Alabama. Choose one of the famous Alabamians from the following list and find Web sites about that person. Does the person have an official Web site? Is there a park or museum with good information about the person? Find three facts about the person that are supported on two different Web sites.

- Hank Aaron, baseball player
- N. Jan Davis, astronaut
- Helen Keller, author and educator
- Coretta Scott King, civil rights leader
- Harper Lee, author
- Rosa Parks, civil rights activist
- Condoleezza Rice, Secretary of State
- Bart Starr, football player
- Hank Williams, musician

LESSON 13: All About Austin

As Bryce and Avaron walked through Austin Bergstrom International Airport, Bryce pointed to a statue and said, "Who is that?"

As the kids approached the statue, Avaron recognized the figure. "Oh, that's Barbara Jordan. She was a remarkable Texan. She was a lawyer, a representative in the U.S. Congress, and a teacher at the University of Texas at Austin."

"I've heard of Barbara Jordan," said Bryce. "She was the first southern African-American woman to serve in the U.S. Congress."

Jordan worked hard for civil rights. She introduced laws to help minority groups and poor people. She was also an amazing orator, or speaker. She became well known for her speech about the value of the U.S. Constitution.

"Where would you like to go first?" Bryce asked.

"Well, since we're in the capital, maybe we should start at the capitol," Avaron replied.

The kids rode the shuttle bus into the center of the city to the pink granite capitol.

"What a beautiful building," said Avaron.

"It's the largest state capitol in the country," Bryce commented.

As the kids entered the building, they passed statues of Stephen F. Austin and Sam Houston. Stephen F. Austin is known as the father of Texas. He helped thousands of colonists settle in Texas when it still belonged to Mexico. He traveled to Mexico City to ask for a separate state government. When this didn't

Barbara Jordan served in the U.S. Congress from 1973 to 1979.

AUSTIN | UNITED STATES

work, he recommended the formation of the state without Mexican permission. For this, he was arrested and held in jail for two years.

Sam Houston also arrived in Texas when it was still a part of Mexico. When the colonists rebelled against Mexican rule, Houston became the commander of the Texan army. He launched a surprise attack on the Mexican leader, General Santa Anna, in the Battle of San Jacinto. As a result of Houston's victory, Texas became an independent country. In 1836, Houston was elected as the first President of the Republic of Texas. Stephen F. Austin served as the Secretary of State. Texas became a state of the United States in 1845.

After wandering throughout the capitol building and around its grassy, tree-covered grounds, the kids went to Zilker Park. This 351-acre park lies in the heart of the city. Bryce and Avaron toured the botanical gardens, rode the miniature train on its three-mile course, and discussed whether to swim or rent a canoe. Avaron wanted to paddle a canoe on Town Lake. Bryce was more interested in swimming at Barton Springs pool. Barton Springs is a spring-fed pool that is over 900 feet long. Its water temperature averages a brisk 68 degrees year-round. Since it was a hot summer day, the kids agreed that it would be best to take a swim. After diving in, Bryce popped up with a stunned expression on his face.

"Wow, there's a big difference between the 98-degree air and this 68-degree water!" he said.

"Brr, it sure gets the blood flowing," agreed Avaron, hopping out after a brief swim.

After relaxing on the grassy hill beside the pool, Bryce thumbed through the guidebook, looking for a good place to eat.

"I've worked up an appetite," he commented.

"I think I know a better way to find a good restaurant," Avaron said.

Bryce put his book down and watched Avaron approach a man and woman sitting nearby. She asked them if they lived in town. When they said yes, she asked them to recommend a place to eat. After chatting for a while, she ran over to her backpack and grabbed a notebook and pen. She made a list of the many places the couple had suggested.

The Texas Capitol was completed in 1888.

Mexican-American War
1846–1848

When Texas was a part of Mexico, its southwest border was the Rio Grande. When Texas became a state, this was the border accepted by the United States. But Mexico said it should be 100 miles to the east at the Nueces River. A border war raged for two years. The war ended in 1848. The agreement with Mexico made the Rio Grande the border and gave the United States California, New Mexico, and parts of Nevada, Utah, Arizona, Colorado, and Wyoming. Mexico in return received $15 million.

AUSTIN | UNITED STATES

"It looks like Austin has a lot of good restaurants," she said, showing Bryce the long list.

"This is my kind of town," he said, laughing.

The kids showered in the changing rooms and walked to a nearby restaurant, where they enjoyed a Tex-Mex meal. Tex-Mex is the Texas version of Mexican food. Instead of the elaborate foods found in the country of Mexico, this regional version of Mexican food is simple. The kids ate tortilla chips served with different kinds of hot sauce. Bryce had an enchilada, which is a corn tortilla filled with meat, vegetables, or cheese and topped with sauce and cheese. Avaron had guacamole (pronounced *gwa-kuh-MO-lee*) salad. Made with mashed avocados, guacamole is seasoned with onion, garlic, lemon, and salt.

"I'm tired of hauling my backpack everywhere," Avaron said. "Let's go check in at the hostel before we do anything else."

After dropping their bags at the hostel and admiring the view of Town Lake, Bryce suggested they go downtown. He wanted to show Avaron something he thought she would enjoy.

The kids walked across the Congress Avenue Bridge, which crosses Town Lake. Avaron admired the view of the capitol, a mile up the road. She followed her brother to where a large group of people sat on a hill.

"What's going on here? The bridge and this hillside are crowded with people," Avaron said.

"You'll find out in just a few minutes," Bryce replied.

Austin is home to the largest urban bat colony in North America. As many as 1.5 million Mexican free-tailed bats live under the Congress Avenue Bridge from March to November. Around dusk each night, they swarm out from under the bridge, where they live in its narrow, vertical spaces.

Avaron was so surprised when the bats began pouring out from underneath the bridge that she sat silently with her mouth wide open.

Bryce laughed and suggested she close her mouth before one of the tiny mammals flew in. He told her all of the facts he had read about the animals.

The bats under the Congress Avenue Bridge migrate from central Mexico, coming to Austin to spend the spring and summer months.

He was especially pleased to report that the bats eat thousands of pounds of insects each night.

"Including pesky mosquitoes," he said, as he slapped one of the bugs that was biting his arm.

The next day, the kids rented bicycles and rode the ten miles of trails that border Town Lake. This Hike and Bike Trail is popular with cyclists, runners, and walkers. As they rounded a bend, they heard music ahead. Families were sitting on the grass listening to a band. The kids stopped for the free concert.

"This seems fitting, since Austin is known as the 'Live Music Capital of the World,'" Bryce commented.

Many people in the crowd wore cowboy hats. While there are still people who work as cowboys today, the time known as the Cowboy Era in Texas lasted from 1866 to 1886. The Spanish first brought horses and cattle into the southwest in the sixteenth century.

"Did you know that cowboys worked about 18 hours a day during the Cowboy Era?" Avaron asked.

"That's a long workday," Bryce commented.

"Most cowboys had small or medium builds, because large men were too heavy for the mustangs. And lots of Texas cowboys were Mexican, African American, and Native American," Avaron said.

"Talking about cowboys makes me think of cows. And thinking of cows makes me think of barbecue," said Bryce.

"Well, we're definitely in the right place for good barbecue," Avaron responded. "*Barbecue* comes from the Spanish word *barbacoa* that means 'a rack of meat hanging over a fire.' Come on, we'll ride a city bus until we smell barbecue cooking."

"And then after we eat, we can ride into the sunset, just like cowboys always do," Bryce laughed.

Mustangs

Mustangs are Spanish horses that were brought to North America hundreds of years ago. Cowboys on Texas cattle ranges used mustangs because the animals were known for their endurance and ability to learn quickly.

Christopher Columbus brought the first cattle to the Western Hemisphere. In 1519, Hernando Cortés brought cattle to Mexico. Many of those cattle wandered to Texas and California.

LESSON 13 — All About Austin

Name _____

Date _____

Traverse the Time Line

Organize events in Texas history on a time line. Use the passage to help you.

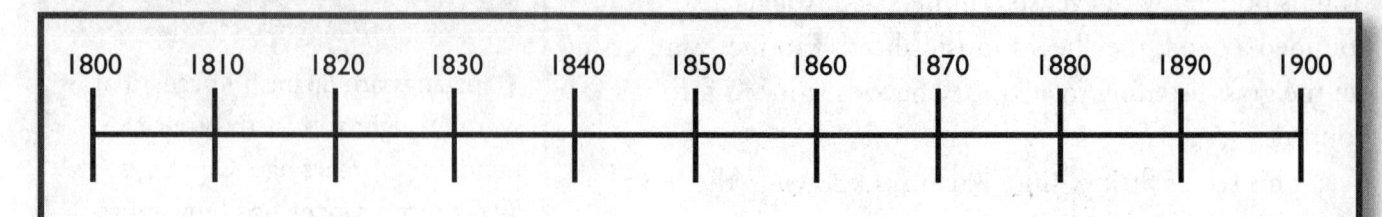

| 1800 | 1810 | 1820 | 1830 | 1840 | 1850 | 1860 | 1870 | 1880 | 1890 | 1900 |

Texas capitol completed

Mexican-American War begins

Mexican-American War ends

Texas becomes a state

Sam Houston becomes President of the Republic of Texas

LESSON 13: All About Austin

Name _____

Date _____

Vocabulary Voyage

| barbecue | botanical | elaborate | formation |
| minority | mustang | orator | rebelled |

Write the vocabulary word from the box that is a synonym for the word or words given.

1. concerning plants _____

2. horse _____

3. grill _____

4. speechmaker _____

Write the vocabulary word from the box that is an antonym for the word given.

5. simple _____

6. majority _____

7. obeyed _____

8. destruction _____

Use each word in the box to write a complete sentence.

_____
_____
_____
_____
_____
_____
_____

www.harcourtschoolsupply.com
© Harcourt Achieve Inc. All rights reserved.

United States: Lesson 13
Journeys Around the World, SV 1419027875

LESSON 13 — All About Austin

Name _____

Date _____

Comprehension Expedition

Darken the circle for the best answer.

1. Why was Stephen F. Austin called the "father of Texas"?
   - Ⓐ He was the first president of the Republic of Texas.
   - Ⓑ He led the army during the Mexican-American War.
   - Ⓒ He helped many Americans settle in the Texas territory.
   - Ⓓ He led the army in the defeat of Santa Anna.

2. What caused the start of the Mexican-American War?
   - Ⓐ Disagreement over the price to pay for a large piece of land in the West
   - Ⓑ Disagreement over the boundary between Texas and Mexico
   - Ⓒ Surprise attack on Santa Anna, the Mexican general
   - Ⓓ Formation of a Texan government separate from Mexico

3. How do you know the seat of Texas government is located in Austin?
   - Ⓐ It is where the capitol is.
   - Ⓑ It is named after Stephen F. Austin.
   - Ⓒ It is considered the Live Music Capital.
   - Ⓓ It is the home of the Congress Avenue Bridge.

Use complete sentences to answer the question.

4. Write a short description of a cowboy working in the cattle industry during the Cowboy Era.

_____
_____
_____
_____
_____
_____
_____
_____

LESSON 13: All About Austin

Name _____

Date _____

Writing Adventure

Sam Houston died in 1863 at the age of 70. Write an obituary for Mr. Houston to run in the Austin newspaper in 1863. Use facts about Houston's life from the passage and from your own research. Be sure to include his contributions to both Tennessee and Texas.

Research Navigation

Houston is the fourth-largest city in the United States and the biggest city in Texas. Imagine that Bryce and Avaron leave Austin and go to Houston for the weekend. What will they do? Use Houston tourism Web sites to find out about this important city. List three things you think Bryce and Avaron will enjoy doing.

Here are some Web sites to get you started.

http://www.visithoustontexas.com/

http://www.houston-guide.com/guide/info/infovisit.html

http://www.houstontravelguide.com/

Lesson 14: Ancient Ruins and Majestic Canyons

"OK, put one knee in Utah, one in Colorado, and then put your hands in Arizona and New Mexico," Avaron said. She was directing Bryce to pose at the Four Corners Monument. He was kneeling at the spot where the corners of the four states meet. This is the only place in the country where the borders of this many states come together.

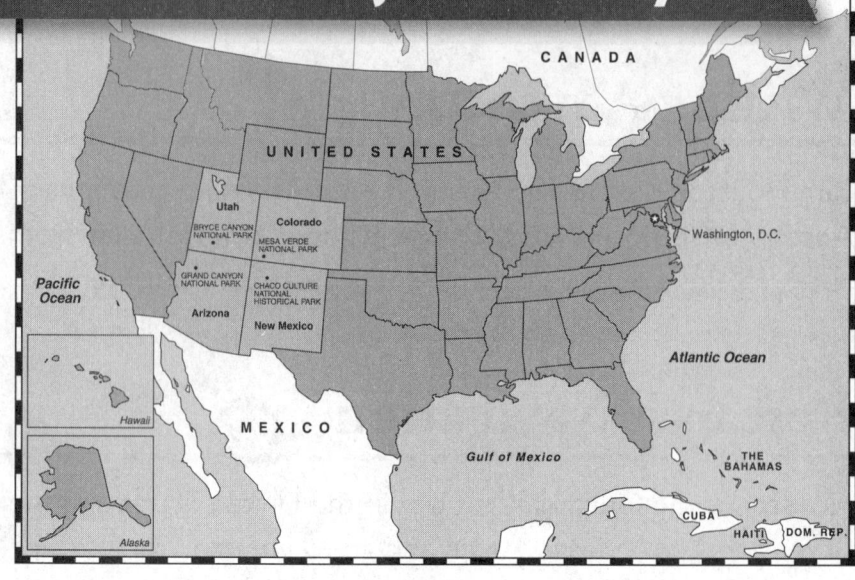

After taking a few photos and looking at the items being sold by Native Americans in the nearby booths, the kids' small tour group boarded the van and drove to Mesa Verde National Park. Located in the southwest corner of Colorado, the park contains ruins of the Pueblo people. They lived in the area from about A.D. 600 to A.D. 1300. During the last hundred years of their occupation of the area, they built elaborate stone villages sheltered by the canyon walls. These remarkable cliff dwellings include Cliff Palace, the largest of the park's groups of houses.

Cliff Palace contains 150 rooms and 23 kivas (pronounced *KEE-vuhs*). Kivas are structures used for ceremonies. They are usually round, and often the main part of the structure is underground. The kiva contained a fire pit, a bench, and a sipapu (pronounced *SEE-pah-puh*). The sipapu is a hole in the kiva floor that represents the navel of the earth. It was believed that the ancient Pueblo people used it to enter this world.

"What a fantastic place," said Avaron.

Cliff Palace is the largest group of buildings in Mesa Verde.

"Yeah, it's beautiful. And we're lucky that the people who used to live here tossed their trash nearby. Studying these artifacts has taught scientists all about the ancient Pueblo people's daily lives," said Bryce.

Bryce had read that the trash piles revealed the people's diet, what their tools were like, and what their pottery looked like. Next, the kids and their tour group went to Balcony House. Accompanied by a park ranger, they climbed a steep ladder. Then they had to crawl through a small passageway to reach the dwelling. Bryce pointed out the original toeholds, or tiny steps, that had been carved into the rock.

"I'm glad we don't have to use those. This ladder is scary enough for me," said their tour leader.

The occupants left Mesa Verde in the late 1200s. While it is unknown exactly why they left, it is likely that a long-term drought was one of the main reasons. It is also possible that centuries of harvest had used up many of the area's natural resources.

The tour's next stop was Chaco Canyon in New Mexico. Now called Chaco Culture National Historical Park, it was a major urban center between A.D. 850 and 1250. Besides buildings, the area had roads, dams, and an irrigation system. The road network covered 400 miles. The center of the culture is called Pueblo Bonita.

"Pueblo Bonita has over 600 rooms and 40 kivas," Bryce noted.

"Imagine the planning that went into this construction," Avaron said.

"Yeah, they knew about architecture, engineering, geometry, landscaping, and astronomy," Bryce commented.

"I hate to admit it, but I didn't know the Native Americans had such advanced civilizations," Avaron said.

"Did you know that this land used to belong to Mexico? If the United States hadn't won the Mexican-American War, we might be in a foreign country right now," Bryce noted.

The Mexican-American War was fought between 1846 and 1848. It was caused by conflicts between the two countries over territory. By the time it ended, the U.S. had gained nearly half of Mexico's land, including California and New Mexico. This helped to reinforce Americans' belief in Manifest Destiny. This was the belief that Americans had the right to expand all the way across North America.

The circular hole is a kiva at the ruins in Chaco Culture National Historical Park.

Manifest Destiny

Manifest Destiny was both a political and a philosophical belief during the nineteenth century. Americans believed it was their divine mission to expand westward and to establish democratic and Protestant ideals.

FOUR CORNERS | UNITED STATES

The tour group proceeded to the Grand Canyon in Arizona. As the kids approached the rim, they were awestruck by how deep the canyon was. They noticed the way the setting sun was changing the colors in the canyon. Some of the rocks contained shades of deep red, pink, and purple.

"I can see why this is considered one of the seven natural wonders of the world," Bryce said.

More than a mile deep and 277 miles long, the Grand Canyon was created by the Colorado River over a period of millions of years. A popular activity among visitors is to ride into the canyon on mules. Bryce and Avaron had arranged to go on one of these trips. A long line of mules, each carrying one person, was led into the canyon by a park employee.

The Grand Canyon is more than a mile deep in some places.

The group started down the Bright Angel Trail. This trail was originally used by the Havasupai Indians as they traveled from the rim down to an area that is now called Indian Garden. The Havasupai people planted squash, corn, and beans here. The planting of these three plants is called "Three Sisters." The cornstalk acts as a pole for the beans to climb. The beans put nutrients in the soil that the corn needs. The squash provide ground cover to keep moisture in the soil. They were able to water the plants with a nearby creek that runs year-round.

After riding for several hours, the group arrived at Phantom Ranch at the bottom of the canyon. The kids went to their cabin and flopped down on their beds.

"I wouldn't have guessed riding a mule could be so tiring," Bryce said.

After eating dinner, the kids went to a ranger program. They learned about the canyon's geology and history. The ranger informed them that some of the rocks in the canyon were four billion years old.

They started the next day with a big breakfast. Then they completed a short hike before climbing back on their mules for the return trip to the canyon rim. A few hours later, a huge shadow briefly blocked the sun above the mule train. Avaron looked up to see what it was.

FOUR CORNERS | UNITED STATES

"Look, it's a California condor!" she exclaimed.

This endangered species was reintroduced into the Grand Canyon in 2001. It is the largest bird in North America. With a wingspan of up to nine and a half feet, it is one of the largest flying birds in the world.

After reaching the rim, the kids joined their tour group again. They ate an early dinner and then returned to the rim to watch the sunset. The changing colors within the canyon and the shadows dancing along its walls made everyone smile.

The following day, the group proceeded to Bryce Canyon in southern Utah. This spectacular park is known for its orange limestone and sandstone pillars that have been shaped by erosion. When something erodes, it is worn away by water, wind, or ice. The stone columns at Bryce Canyon are called hoodoos.

As the kids hiked along one of the trails, Bryce pointed to a hoodoo. He said, "That one looks like a person."

"The Paiute Indians had a legend about the hoodoos. They said the rocks were formed when the people who used to live here were turned to stone as punishment for bad behavior," Avaron commented.

Native Americans lived in the area around Bryce Canyon for thousands of years. Mormon settlers arrived in the 1850s. One of the settlers was Ebenezer Bryce. The park was named after him. The area did not get much rain, so the settlers dug a ten-mile-long canal from the Sevier River so that they could water their crops.

"Maybe you were named after Ebenezer Bryce. I think I'll start calling you 'Ebenezer.' Would you like that?" Avaron asked jokingly.

Bryce ignored her. "The orange rocks are so striking against the brilliant blue sky," he said.

Avaron turned in a full circle, studying the landscape. "This place is magical. It's my favorite stop so far in the southwest," she said.

Bryce Canyon's natural rock pillars are called hoodoos.

Mormons

Mormons are a Christian group that was founded in 1830 by Joseph Smith. The religion began in New York, but the Mormons moved to the far west to escape unfair treatment because of their religion. They settled near the Great Salt Lake in present-day Utah, where they founded Salt Lake City.

LESSON 14: Ancient Ruins and Majestic Canyons

Name _____

Date _____

Chart the Course

Activities Available in Southwestern U.S. National Parks

National Park	Bird-Watching	Camping	Cross-Country Skiing	Hiking	Interpretive Programs	Nature Walks	Snowshoeing	Horseback Riding	Campground	Lodge	Museum	Visitor Center
Mesa Verde, Colorado	X	X	X	X	X	X	X		1	1	1	1
Chaco Culture, New Mexico		X		X		X			1		1	1
Grand Canyon, Arizona	X	X	X	X	X	X	X	X	4	7	2	1
Bryce Canyon, Utah	X	X	X	X	X	X	X	X	2	1		1
Petrified Forest, Arizona				X	X	X		X			1	2
Zion, Utah	X	X		X	X			X	3	1	1	2

Use the table to answer the questions.

1. Which park has the most campgrounds? _____

2. Which parks allow snowshoeing? _____

3. You would like to go to a park and stay in a lodge and go cross-country skiing. Which of these parks might you go to? _____

4. You would like to go bird-watching, snowshoeing, and camping in Arizona. Where might you go? _____

5. Using the information in the passage, why do you think there is no horseback riding in Mesa Verde and Chaco Culture parks? _____

LESSON 14: Ancient Ruins and Majestic Canyons

Name _____
Date _____

Vocabulary Voyage

Write "True" if the statement is true. Write "False" if the statement is not true. Context clues in the passage provide help for the boldfaced words.

1. The Pueblos built **cliff dwellings** near canyon walls. _____

2. Farming is the main occupation in an **urban** area. _____

3. Many years of **erosion** caused rock and soil to wear away. _____

4. People who believed in **Manifest Destiny** believed they should conquer all of North America from the Atlantic to the Pacific oceans. _____

5. A study of **geology** teaches history through a study of rocks. _____

6. Park rangers built **toeholds** to slide down the side of a cliff. _____

7. The **Pueblo** people built homes from logs and sod. _____

8. A spiritual ceremony was held in the **kiva**. _____

Rewrite each false statement to make it a true statement.

_____
_____
_____
_____
_____
_____
_____
_____
_____

LESSON 14
Ancient Ruins and Majestic Canyons

Name _____

Date _____

Comprehension Expedition

Darken the circle for the best answer.

1. How did the concept of Manifest Destiny affect the United States's relationship with Mexico?
   - Ⓐ It harmed the relationship because it caused a war over some of Mexico's land.
   - Ⓑ It helped the relationship because Mexico wanted to give away large parts of its land.
   - Ⓒ It helped the relationship because Mexico wanted the United States to grow bigger.
   - Ⓓ It harmed the relationship because Americans took jobs away from Mexicans.

2. How did present-day scientists learn about ancient Pueblo life in the Mesa Verde region of Colorado?
   - Ⓐ They read books left behind by the Pueblo people.
   - Ⓑ They found answers in the sipapu.
   - Ⓒ They interviewed the people who lived in the area.
   - Ⓓ They studied trash the Pueblo people left behind.

3. What is NOT an advantage of Three Sisters gardening?
   - Ⓐ It doesn't need a lot of maintenance.
   - Ⓑ It makes a big variety of crops.
   - Ⓒ It keeps water in the soil.
   - Ⓓ It doesn't use much land.

Use complete sentences to answer the question.

4. How do you know American Indians lived in the area where Bryce Canyon National Park is?

_____
_____
_____
_____
_____
_____
_____

LESSON 14
Ancient Ruins and Majestic Canyons

Name _____

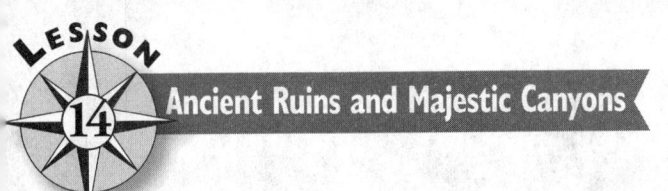

Date _____

Writing Adventure

Choose two national parks described in the passage or two that you know about. Write three paragraphs to compare and contrast the two parks. Include physical features, history, and available activities.

Research Navigation

Many different kinds of people settled the American West in the 1800s. Go to the Web site below for a list of people who had an influence in the westward expansion of America.

http://www.pbs.org/weta/thewest/people/

- Choose one name from the list and read the biography.

- Did this person have a positive or a negative effect on life in the American West?

LESSON 15: A City by the Bay: San Francisco

"I don't want to tour a big city. It's too much of a jolt after our time enjoying the beauty of the southwest. I'd rather enjoy nature than a bunch of big buildings," Bryce grumbled.

"I'm betting that there are lots of reasons that San Francisco is one of the most-visited cities in the United States. And you might even enjoy your visit here," Avaron replied.

The kids boarded a cable car. Avaron read aloud from her guidebook.

"The first cable car ran in San Francisco in 1873. The cars are pulled along tracks after latching onto a moving cable that is under the street. Cable cars have the ability to climb the city's many steep hills. Along with being a form of public transportation, they have become an important tourist attraction."

She looked at Bryce. He had a bored expression on his face. The kids got off the cable car when they arrived at Fisherman's Wharf.

"Let's go eat fresh seafood for lunch," Avaron suggested.

"The crowds are terrible. I wish I were in the desert again," Bryce moaned.

After being seated, Bryce looked around to determine where the loud barking noises he heard were coming from. Avaron pointed to the dozens of sea lions basking on the pier outside.

"Cool! I've never seen so many sea lions in one place! What is that island over there?" Bryce asked.

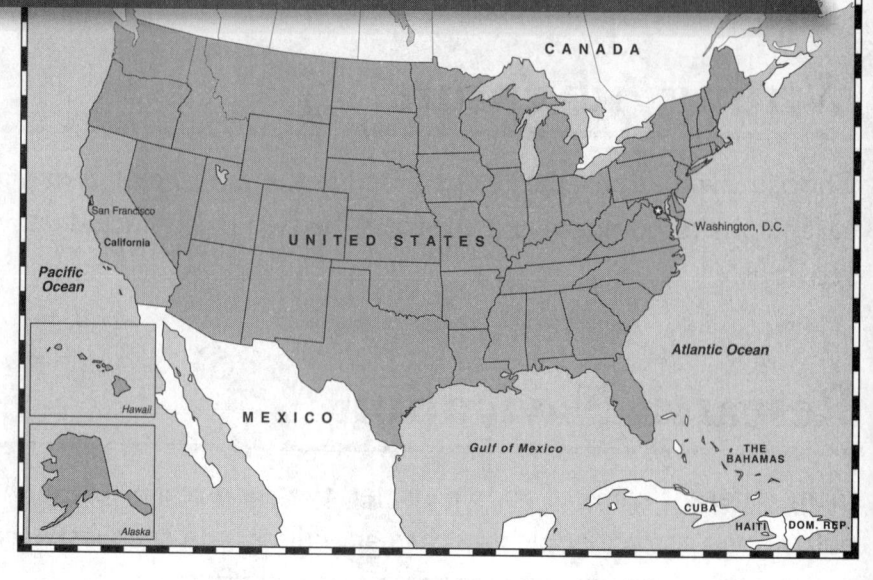

Cable cars are so important to San Francisco that there is a Cable Car Museum in town.

SAN FRANCISCO | UNITED STATES

"That's Alcatraz. It was a federal prison from 1934 to 1963," Avaron replied.

"Really, that's Alcatraz? I've read about it. I didn't remember that it was in San Francisco Bay. I wonder if we can take a tour," Bryce said excitedly.

"We can check at the ticket booths down on the pier after we eat. There are lots of tour boats that leave from Fisherman's Wharf every day," Avaron replied.

After finishing their meal, the kids went to a ticket booth. Bryce asked about booking a tour. The ticket agent told him all the tours were sold out.

When he turned around to tell Avaron, she handed him a ticket for a boat that was scheduled to leave in fifteen minutes. In answer to his stunned expression, she explained that she had reserved the tickets several days earlier.

After making the mile-and-a-half trip to the island, the tourists were greeted by a park ranger. She explained that Alcatraz Island was the site of the first lighthouse on the California coast. She told them that army troops had been stationed there a few years later in 1859. Then the island served as a military prison. Beginning in 1934, Alcatraz was a federal prison for some of the country's most dangerous prisoners.

The tour group entered the prison to see the cellblock. The cells were five feet by nine feet, and prisoners spent 23 hours a day inside them. They had to earn extra time outside for work and recreation.

"Is it true that no one ever escaped from Alcatraz?" Bryce asked.

The ranger replied, "Actually, several people attempted to escape, but many were caught or killed in the process. A few others disappeared and were never heard from again, so it is assumed that they drowned in the cold water and fast currents that surround the island."

After boarding the boat again, the kids enjoyed riding underneath the Golden Gate Bridge. This famous suspension bridge was a major engineering achievement. Construction began in 1933. Building in the middle of an ocean

Nicknamed "The Rock," Alcatraz sits in San Francisco Bay.

The Golden Gate Bridge is 1.7 miles long and is painted orange.

SAN FRANCISCO | UNITED STATES

channel known for its rough waters presented many challenges. In 1936, a huge net was hung below the bridge to save workers who fell. This gave the men much more confidence, and they began to work faster. The bridge was completed in 1937.

The kids returned to the pier, and Avaron led the way to her next surprise destination. Aquarium of the Bay teaches visitors about the varied life found in San Francisco Bay. A 300-foot-long tunnel under the water allows visitors to see the sharks, eels, and octopus that live here. A series of pools inside the aquarium are set up so that visitors can actually touch the rays and sharks.

"That was amazing," said Bryce. "I've never petted a shark before."

The kids returned to their hostel to sleep. The following morning, they went to Chinatown. Home to about 30,000 Chinese people, it is one of the largest Chinese communities outside of China.

"Chinese people played a major role in building the first transcontinental railroad in the U.S. When the railroad was completed, people could travel across the country in about six days instead of the six months it used to take when traveling by wagon," Bryce commented.

"It sounds almost like you've become interested in San Francisco," Avaron replied.

Bryce continued, "The railroad was completed in 1869. Workers endured freezing weather in the mountains, hot weather in the deserts, and working with dynamite on steep mountainsides. To make matters even more difficult, the Chinese laborers were not treated fairly. White workers were paid more and given shelter and food. Chinese workers made several dollars less per month and had to provide their own tents and food."

Chinatown is a neighborhood in San Francisco about eight blocks long.

SAN FRANCISCO | UNITED STATES

"Yeah, and then in 1882, the Chinese Exclusion Act was passed. This suspended immigration for a number of years," Avaron commented.

The kids wandered down the narrow alleys of Chinatown. They entered a small factory where fortune cookies were made. Two women sat beside small metal pans. After the dough was squirted into the pan by a machine, they scooped up the round cookies and folded them in half with a paper fortune inside. The women then placed the still-warm dough over a small metal bar so that the cookie hardened with the fortune inside. The kids enjoyed free samples and then bought a bag of the cookies to take with them.

Their next stop was Russian Hill. This is one of the city's many residential neighborhoods. They climbed up Lombard Street just so they could look back down on it from above. Known as the "world's crookedest street," it contains many sharp curves that made it possible for traffic to travel up and down the steep hill.

"I read that Russian Hill got its name when gold miners found a cemetery where some Russians were buried at the top of the hill," Bryce noted.

The California Gold Rush began in 1848. Most of the gold was found in the nearby towns of Stockton and Sacramento. Located between the towns, San Francisco was where most prospectors started off. It was also where many incoming ships landed. The city's population boomed. This is when many of the Chinese immigrants first arrived. They started out as gold miners and later became railroad workers.

Next, the kids went to the Golden Gate National Recreation Area. One of the largest urban national parks in the world, it contains miles of bay and ocean shoreline. It also has archaeological sites, old forts, and lots of wildlife. Hawks, seabirds, coyotes, and deer are frequently seen by visitors.

"We could spend days in here and still not see everything," Avaron commented.

"Yeah, this is amazing," Bryce said.

By late afternoon, fog was moving in. A common occurrence in San Francisco, the fog made faraway things disappear. The kids could no longer see Alcatraz Island. Avaron stopped to take photos.

"Even the fog is beautiful here," she said.

"I knew this was going to be a cool city!" Bryce exclaimed.

Earthquakes

Along with its fog, San Francisco is known for its earthquakes. The city was severely damaged by a quake in 1906. More recent quakes have resulted in damage as well. California sits where two tectonic plates meet. These shifting sections of the earth's crust create mountains and volcanoes, as well as causing earthquakes.

Muir Woods

Just two miles from the Golden Gate National Recreation Area lies Muir Woods. This park contains the tallest type of tree in the world, the 1,000-year-old coast redwood. The coast redwood stands 260 feet high. This small forest of giant trees shows visitors what now-developed Marin County once looked like.

LESSON 15
A City by the Bay: San Francisco

Name _____

Date _____

Chart the Course

Use the pie charts to answer each question.

1. How has immigration from Latin American countries changed since 1900?

   _____
   _____
   _____

2. What might be one reason immigration from Asia was only 1.2 percent in 1900? (Use the passage to help you.)

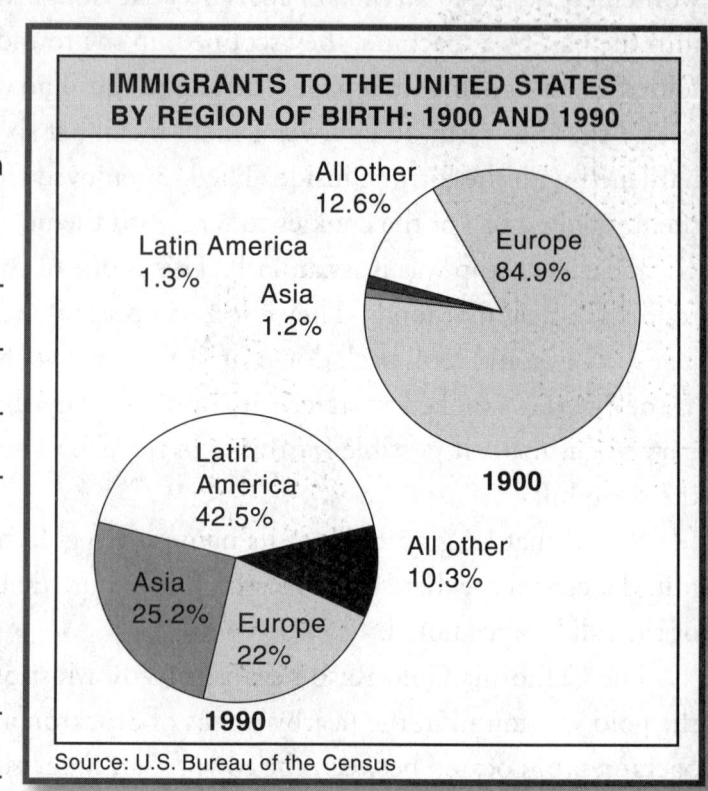

   _____
   _____
   _____

IMMIGRANTS TO THE UNITED STATES BY REGION OF BIRTH: 1900 AND 1990

1900:
- Europe 84.9%
- All other 12.6%
- Latin America 1.3%
- Asia 1.2%

1990:
- Latin America 42.5%
- Asia 25.2%
- Europe 22%
- All other 10.3%

Source: U.S. Bureau of the Census

3. How has immigration from Europe changed since 1900?

   _____
   _____

4. What language did most of the immigrants to the United States speak in 1990?

   _____

5. In 1900 most immigrants to the United States arrived by ship. What modes of transportation might immigrants use today?

   _____
   _____
   _____

LESSON 15
A City by the Bay: San Francisco

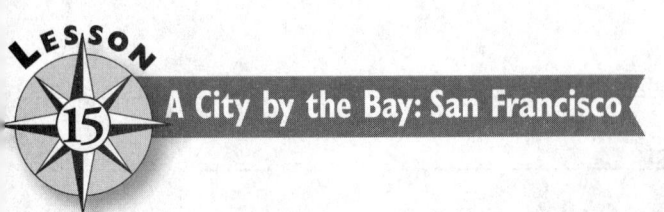

Name _____
Date _____

Vocabulary Voyage

Use the words in the box and the clues to complete the puzzle.

| cellblock | current | suspension bridge |
| destination | tectonic plates | transcontinental |

Down

1. a place where someone is going; the goal of a journey
2. pieces of the earth's crust that can move
5. a movement of water in one direction

Across

3. a division in a prison made up of several cells
4. extending across the continent from coast to coast
6. a bridge that is supported by cables hung from towers

LESSON 15
A City by the Bay: San Francisco

Name _____
Date _____

Comprehension Expedition

Darken the circle for the best answer.

1. What made many Chinese people settle in San Francisco?
   Ⓐ They came to build the railroad and cable car system.
   Ⓑ They came to mine for gold and later to work on the railroad.
   Ⓒ They came as prisoners at Alcatraz.
   Ⓓ They came because a law was passed in 1882.

2. Where might a visitor go to see what the area around San Francisco looked like before the Gold Rush?
   Ⓐ Alcatraz
   Ⓑ Muir Woods
   Ⓒ Russian Hill
   Ⓓ Chinatown

3. How did the transcontinental railroad change the United States?
   Ⓐ It brought more settlement to the western region.
   Ⓑ It made San Francisco a major port city.
   Ⓒ It brought many prospectors west in search of gold.
   Ⓓ It brought more European immigration to the country.

Use complete sentences to answer the question.

4. Why was Alcatraz a good place for a prison?

_____
_____
_____
_____
_____
_____
_____

LESSON 15
A City by the Bay: San Francisco

Name _____

Date _____

Writing Adventure

California is home to the major American cities of Los Angeles, San Francisco, San Diego, and Oakland. Pick one California city and write the name vertically on a sheet of paper. Use each letter in the city name as the first letter in a line of poetry about that city. You may use reference books or the Internet to learn more about the city you chose.

Research Navigation

There are 21 Spanish missions in California. Use the Internet to learn more about the missions. Research to find the following information.

1. Who built and lived in the missions?

2. Which mission is the farthest south? Which is the farthest north?

3. What are the missions used for today?

4. Mark the 21 missions on a map of California.

Here are some Web sites to get you started.

> http://library.thinkquest.org/3615/
> http://missionsofcalifornia.org/missions/index.html

Answer Key

Lesson 1: Baja by Bus

page 10
1. Gulf of California
2. San Diego
3. 200 miles; about 3 h 20 min
4. Ciudad Victoria
5. Gulf of Mexico

page 11
1. lengthwise
2. civilization
3. pyramid
4. constitution
5. migrate
6. peninsula
7. lagoon
8. evaporate
Spanish, peso, Guatemala

page 12
1. B
2. D
3. A
4. Salt is commonly used in food preparation, so there is a demand for it. Salt that is harvested can be sold throughout the world.

Lesson 2: A Little Dog and a Big State

page 18
1. Chihuahua
2. México
3. Federal District
4. Baja California Sur; Baja California
5. Oregon

page 19
1. nomad
2. missionary
3. habitation
4. gorge
5. converting
6. elevation
Sentences will vary.

page 20
1. D
2. A
3. A
4. Silver was mined there in the 1700s. Missionaries arrived there in the 1600s.

Lesson 3: Aztecs and Art in Mexico City

page 26
1. 286 years
2. Aztecs
3. Aztecs
4. Aztecs
5. 6 years

page 27
1. destruction
2. metropolitan
3. pre-Columbian
4. banquet
5. anthropology
6. astronomy
7. mural
8. chinampas
Sentences will vary.

page 28
1. C
2. A
3. B
4. Possible answer: Religion was the cornerstone of the Aztec civilization. Evidence of this is found in all aspects of the people's lives. The center of their civilization, Tenochtitlán, was chosen based on their religious beliefs. They built large and beautiful temples. Their calendar had a religious symbol in the center. Their art depicted many religious symbols.

Lesson 4: Jalisco Holiday

page 34
1. Teatro Degollado; Avaron
2. northwest
3. A. Museo de la Ciudad; B. Palacio de Justicia; C. Monumento a la Independencia

page 35
1. sombreros
2. flan
3. mariachi
4. huaraches
5. cathedral
6. charro
Sentences will vary.

page 36
1. B
2. C
3. D
4. The Huichol Indians of the mountains near Puerto Vallarta are believed to be descendants of the Aztecs.

Lesson 5: Reefs, Ruins, and Jaguars

page 42
1–4. Students will accurately mark areas on the map.
5. Gulf of Mexico, Pacific Ocean

page 43
1. asteroid
2. extinction
3. impact
4. biologist
5. deities
6. decapitated
7. cenotes
8. architecture
Sentences will vary.

page 44
1. D
2. D
3. A
4. Possible answers: Building, because they were able to construct large temples and pyramids. Astronomy, because they were able to make a calendar and buildings that created artistic shadows at certain times of the year. Art, since they made stone carvings on their buildings.

Lesson 6: Walking in Viking Footsteps

page 50
1. Ontario
2. Yukon Territory and Nunavut; Possible answer: Because they are so far north that the weather makes it difficult for people to live there.
3. Nunavut
4. Pacific coast

page 51
1. glacier
2. iceberg
3. provinces and territories
4. sod
5. bog
6. Inuit
7. parliamentary democracy
Sentences will vary.

page 52
1. C
2. A
3. B
4. provinces and territories; states
5. Canada has a prime minister who is the head of the government. However, the queen of England is the chief of state. In the United States, the president is both the head of the government and the chief of state.
6. They both have a history of being colonized by the British.

Lesson 7: Mostly Québec

page 58
1. Alberta and Saskatchewan
2. Yukon Territory, Northwest Territories
3. fish, trees, natural gas
4. coal mining

page 59
Across
1. channel
5. sightseeing
7. hydroelectric
8. obligate
Down
2. ecosystem
3. incline
4. angle
6. generate

page 60
1. B
2. B
3. D
4. Possible answers: It produces electricity by means of hydroelectric plants. It brings in many tourists whose dollars contribute to the economy.

Lesson 8: Manitoba in the Middle

page 66
1. dry, highland, mild, cold, and polar
2. cold
3. mild
4. The northern part has primarily a cold and dry polar climate, and the southern part has a mix of mild, highland, dry, and cold, depending on location.
5. Whitehorse, Yellowknife, Edmonton, Regina, Winnipeg, Ottawa, Québec, and St. John's

page 67
1. Hudson's Bay Company
2. Aboriginal
3. Dioramas
4. Immigrants
5. Perogies
6. Petroforms
7. Bison
8. Métis
Sentences will vary.

page 68
1. C
2. D
3. A
4. It has a holiday that honors aboriginal groups.

Lesson 9: The Beauty of British Columbia

page 74
1. Halifax
2. Iqaluit; Winnipeg
3. They both receive the same amount of snow and almost the same amount of rain.
4. Possible answers: Indoor sports such as bowling or basketball and snow sports such as skiing and snowboarding.
5. Answers will vary.

page 75
1. dim sum
2. orca
3. woolly mammoth
4. totem pole
5. potlatch
6. dense
7. provincial
Sentences will vary.

page 76
1. B
2. B
3. D
4. Europeans introduced First Peoples to metal and Christianity.

Lesson 10: Yukon Territory: Gold Rush

page 82
1–5. Students will accurately mark areas on the map.

page 83
1. avalanche
2. harsh
3. prospector
4. customs duties
5. provisions
6. artifacts
7. shortage
8. musher
9. tributaries
Sentences will vary.

page 84
1. C
2. D
3. B
4. They respond to voice commands, and the musher does not use reins or leashes.

Lesson 11: A City Without a State

page 90
1. East Coast
2. Canadian Core
3. San Francisco, Los Angeles, San Diego, Tijuana
4. They are all located on the coast (or on water).
5. Possible answer: They all lie on or near water. Possible answers might include climate, jobs, scenic areas.

page 91
1. legislators
2. capital
3. impeach
4. executive
5. legislative
6. capitol
7. Congress
8. veto
9. judicial
Dolley Madison

page 92
1. A
2. C
3. B
4. Possible answer: Each branch checks the other branches. The executive branch approves or vetoes all laws coming from the legislative branch. The judicial branch can override any laws signed by the president. The legislative branch can remove judges or the president.

Lesson 12: Exploring the Deep South: Alabama

page 98
1. Texas, Louisiana, Mississippi, Georgia, South Carolina, Florida
2. It was the capital of the Confederacy.
3. none
4. Possible answer: Alabama was located in the center of the Confederacy and was located on the Gulf.
5. Texas

page 99
1. kudzu
2. sit-in
3. seceded
4. segregated
5. equality
6. boycott
7. resistance
8. civil disobedience

page 100
1. D
2. A
3. B
4. The Supreme Court ruled to end segregation. People against the ruling reacted violently. The ruling also opened doors for demonstrations against unfair laws and the civil rights movement.

Lesson 13: All About Austin

page 106
Students will put the following events in this order on the time line:
1836 Sam Houston becomes President of the Republic of Texas
1845 Texas becomes a state
1846 Mexican-American War begins
1848 Mexican-American War ends
1888 Texas capitol completed

page 107
1. botanical
2. mustang
3. barbecue
4. orator
5. elaborate
6. minority
7. rebelled
8. formation
Sentences will vary.

page 108
1. C
2. B
3. A
4. Answers might include that it would be a man of short to medium build who was good with horses and willing to work 18 hours a day.

Lesson 14: Ancient Ruins and Majestic Canyons

page 114
1. Grand Canyon
2. Mesa Verde, Grand Canyon, Bryce Canyon
3. Mesa Verde, Grand Canyon, or Bryce Canyon
4. Grand Canyon
5. Both are sites of Native American ruins. Horses could trample on artifacts or other historical evidence.

page 115
1. True
2. False
3. True
4. True
5. True
6. False
7. False
8. True

Answers will vary. Suggested:
2. Farming is the main occupation in a rural area.
6. The Pueblo people built toeholds to climb up and down the side of a cliff.
7. The Pueblo people built cliff dwellings.

page 116
1. A
2. D
3. B
4. They created a legend about the rock formations there.

Lesson 15: A City by the Bay: San Francisco

page 122
1. It became 40 times greater in 1990 than in 1900.
2. The 1882 Chinese Exclusion Act stopped immigration from China for a number of years.
3. It has decreased to about $\frac{1}{4}$ of what it was in 1900.
4. Spanish
5. Possible answers: automobile, airplane

page 123
Down
1. destination
2. tectonic plates
5. current

Across
3. cellblock
4. transcontinental
6. suspension bridge

page 124
1. B
2. B
3. A
4. It is surrounded by water and would be hard for prisoners to escape.

Harcourt Achieve Inc. is not responsible for the content of any Web site listed in this book except its own. All material contained on these sites is the responsibility of the hosts and creators. The Web site addresses are current as of the date of publication.

Photo Acknowledgments

P.15 ©Robert Frerck/Odyssey Productions, Chicago; p.16 ©Sami Sarkis/The Stock Solution; p.31 ©QT Luong/terragalleria.com; p. 63 ©Bill Brooks/Alamy; p.64b ©Parks Canada; p.94, 97b, 103, 110, 112, 113 ©Constance D. Israel; p. 96, 97t, 102 ©Library of Congress.

Additional photography by Comstock Royalty Free; Corbis Royalty Free; Corel Royalty Free; Digital Vision/Getty Images; Dreamstime; IndexOpen; Morguefile; PhotoDisc/Getty Images Royalty Free; Photos.com; ShutterStock; Stockbyte Royalty Free; Wikipedia/Wikimedia; Wonderfile.